Mama, YOU BE THE DIFFERENCE

A BIBLE STUDY FOR MOMS BY MOMS

JESSIE SENECA

Unless otherwise noted, Scripture quotations are taken from the New American Standard Bible (NASB) © 1960, 1962, 1963, 1968, 1971, 1972, 1973, 1975, 1977, 1995 by The Lockman Foundation. Used by permission.

Scripture quotations marks ESV are taken from The ESV® Bible (The Holy Bible, English Standard Version®). ESV® Text Edition: 2016. Copyright © 2001 by Crossway, a publishing ministry of Good News Publishers. The ESV® text has been reproduced in cooperation with and by permission of Good News Publishers. Unauthorized reproduction of this publication is prohibited. All rights reserved.

Scripture quotations marked HCSB are taken from the Holman Christian Standard Bible®. Copyright © 1999, 2000, 2002, 2003, 2009 by Holman Bible Publishers. Used with permission by Holman Bible Publishers, Nashville, Tennessee. All rights reserved.

Scripture quotations marked MSG are taken from THE MESSAGE. Copyright © by Eugene Peterson 1993, 1994, 1995, 1996, 2000, 2001, 2002. Used by permission of NavPress Publishing Group.

Scripture quotations marked NET are taken from the New English Translation (net) net Bible ® copyright ©1196–2006 by Biblical Studies Press, L.L.C., http://netbible.com. All rights reserved.

Scripture quotations marked NIV are taken from the Holy Bible, New International Version®. NIV®. Copyright © 1973, 1978, 1984, 2011 by Biblica, Inc.™ Used by permission. All rights reserved worldwide.

Scripture quotations marked NLT are taken from the Holy Bible. New Living Translation copyright© 1996, 2004, 2007 by Tyndale House Foundation. Used by permission of Tyndale House Publishers, Inc. Carol Stream, Illinois 60188. All rights reserved.

Scripture quotations marked TLB are taken from The Living Bible copyright © 1971 by Tyndale House Foundation. Used by permission of Tyndale House Publishers Inc., Carol Stream, Illinois 60188. All rights reserved. The Living Bible, TLB, and the The Living Bible logo are registered trademarks of Tyndale House Publishers.

Scripture quotations marked TPT are from The Passion Translation®. Copyright © 2017, 2018 by Passion & Fire Ministries, Inc. Used by permission. All rights reserved. ThePassionTranslation.com.All websites, internet addresses, and book titles are offered as a resource. They are not intended in any way to be or imply an endorsement of the publisher.

All emphasis in Scripture is the author's.

Editing by Christy Distler, Avodah Editorial Services
Book cover and interior design and typesetting by Lisa Von De Linde of LisaVdesigns.com
Author photo by Ryan O. Photography

Published by Bright Communications LLC, BrightCommunications.net

ISBN: 978-1-961198-07-4

Printed in the United States of America

To my daughters, Lauren and Sarah.

I have learned more about motherhood from watching you.

You have given me the greatest gift—becoming a mimi.

Thank you for the privilege of being your mom.

Love you to the moon and back.

TABLE OF CONTENTS

A NOTE FROM JESSIE

Welcome to the Bible study, *Mama, You Be The Difference*, a study for moms by moms.

My quest for encouraging moms came in 2017, while I was writing *Raising Girls: Diaper to Diamond*. The question at the forefront of my mind was, What do I wish the younger me knew? That same question continued to guide me as I wrote this study.

Through speaking at mom conferences and churches where I've met so many moms, I quickly realized they were hungry to hear directly from God through the reading of His Word. I also know the impact that reading God's Word daily has had in my own life, and this compelled me to write this study. My desire is to help you realize the difference God makes in your life, and in turn the difference you'll make in the lives of your family by living with inspired purpose every day as a result of embracing biblical truths applicable to motherhood.

In my years of ministry, I've been so blessed to meet some amazing women who have the same desire to help women embrace God's Word as truth and see the influence it has on their lives. I've asked them to contribute to the daily work in the section "Let's Hear from Others." Here you'll find practical tips and be encouraged through personal stories of women who've gone before you on the motherhood journey.

How to Use This Study

Let me first say that I'm so thankful you've picked up this book!

You can work through this study on your own or with a group of friends. Either way, you'll meet God on the pages of His holy Word and be inspired to live a life fully committed to Him.

Mama, You Be The Difference is a five-week study with five days of written work for each week. Each day, you'll have Scripture to look up and an application to help you live a purpose-filled life and be encouraged in your motherhood walk. No matter whether you're a first-time mom or a mom who now has grandchildren, you'll grow in your relationship with God.

At the end of each day:

1. You'll hear from another mom in the "Let's Hear from Others" section. You'll also read practical tips and be encouraged through personal stories of seasoned moms.

2. The "Action Step" section provides prompts you can consider applying to your day or week. This is totally optional, but doing it will help you personalize what you learned during that day in a tangible way.

3. The "Prayer" section will help you complete the day's study.

4. The "Write Out Your Thoughts" section provides space for you to record what God has placed on your heart. For example, you can journal your thoughts, write out the main point you learned that day, or pen a personal prayer to God.

Second Timothy 2:15 is the key verse of this study: "Be diligent to present yourself approved to God as a workman who does not need to be ashamed, accurately handling the word of truth." Being diligent by presenting yourself to God will impact not only your life but the lives of those around you.

My prayer is that your life will be transformed through a living encounter with God as you meet Him on the pages of His holy written Word.

Journeying with Him,

WEEK ONE

It's not always the
big moments that mark
our days, but the small
moments that link
them together.

JESSIE SENECA

Day One

YOU BE THE DIFFERENCE

Be diligent to present yourself approved
to God as a workman who does not need to be ashamed,
accurately handling the word of truth.

2 TIMOTHY 2:15

Welcome to the *Mama, You Be the Difference* Bible study! I look forward to spending the next five weeks with you as you journey through the precepts of God's Word, seek parenting skills, and become a wiser woman. While this book doesn't have the power to make you the perfect mom, it can help you become a mom who lives with purpose. So let's get going.

Oh, wait. One more word of encouragement. I've done my fair share of Bible studies, and sometimes I've wanted to set the study aside halfway through. If this happens to you, please, please do your best to see this book through to the end. It will be worth it, resilient Mom!

I'm not sure where you find yourself as you pick up this study. You could be expecting your first bundle of joy, you may have received your long-awaited child through adoption, you may be multiple kids into this parenting thing, or you may be through the hands-on parenting season and find yourself praying for your adult children and maybe some grandkids. Just for the record, moms are never really out of the parenting scene; our roles just look different. New seasons of parenting await.

No matter where you find yourself, it starts with you. You can be the difference. Your kids are watching you, which means you're a living, breathing representation of God's love. I don't say this to bring shame, condemnation, or guilt, but as a reminder and an encouragement. Your role is so important! *You* are so important.

Much of what I'm going to share throughout this study are things I wish I could tell the younger me. My prayer is that you'll read this book with an open mind, heart, and spirit. The experiences shared by me and the other women can help you see ways to become a better version of yourself.

Believe me when I say this: I am terrified of tackling this topic. I need you to know right from the get-go, I am not an expert, and I have not done it all right. I can't give you a formula to have it all turn out pretty. Goodness, there were days I would stand drenched in the shower, not knowing if the water was from the shower head or the waterfall of tears streaming down my face as I asked God, "Can we start this whole motherhood and parenting thing over again?"

Motherhood is not for the faint of heart. So hang in there and hang on. It's a journey.

On this first day, I want to start with you, Mom. Many times, moms think it's not "all about me"—but today, yes, it's all about you!

Read the following Scripture passages and circle the words *you, your,* and *yourself.*

Only give heed to yourself and keep your soul diligently, so that you do not forget the things which your eyes have seen and they do not depart from your heart all the days of your life; but make them known to your sons and your grandsons.... So watch yourselves carefully.... So watch yourselves, that you do not forget the covenant of the Lord your God which He made with you, and make for yourselves a graven image in the form of anything against which the Lord your God has commanded you.... But from there you will seek the Lord your God, and you will find Him if you search for Him with all your heart and soul. (Deuteronomy 4:9, 15, 23, 29)

Be diligent to present yourself approved to God as a workman who does not need to be ashamed, accurately handling the word of truth. (2 Timothy 2:15)

> Therefore, I urge you, brothers and sisters, in view of God's mercy, to offer your bodies as a living sacrifice, holy and pleasing to God—this is your true and proper worship. Do not conform to the pattern of this world, but be transformed by the renewing of your mind. Then you will be able to test and approve what God's will is—his good, pleasing and perfect will. (Romans 12:1–2 NIV)

In these passages, Moses is instructing the nation of Israel, and Paul is instructing his son in the faith, Timothy, and the church in Rome, of the importance of caring for themselves. And the same is true for you. You must care for yourself before caring for others. I know some days that's really hard, like when you realize it's three in the afternoon and you still haven't brushed your teeth. Mama said there'd be days like this, right? But you must carve out time to focus on yourself, and that's why I'm so glad you are doing this study—to strengthen you and help you be the best mama you can be.

> Moms must have the life-giving connection to God before we can try to help others. Otherwise, we're trying to share limited, frazzled resources, and that's the quickest way to burn out.

If you've done any flying, you know that before the airplane even takes off, flight attendants spend several minutes discussing safety protocols. One of the safety items is the oxygen mask and how to handle it if needed. If the oxygen masks drop down, that means the cabin pressure is off. You can lose consciousness very quickly without the proper amount of air. If you're traveling with someone who needs help with a mask, like a child or an elderly person, you're instructed to put on your own mask first so you don't lose consciousness before you can help those around you.

Just like in this analogy, moms must have the life-giving connection to God before we can try to help others. Otherwise, we're trying to share limited, frazzled resources, and that's the quickest way to burn out.

Now, let's get to some thought-provoking questions right out of the gate.

What are some qualities you want your kids to recognize in you?

What are some ways you try to exhibit these qualities? Do you attempt to display them in your own strength?

Read Galatians 5:22–26 and record the nine qualities represented in the fruit of the Spirit. Then, next to each quality, note the ones you're doing well with and those you need additional help with.

You be the living difference of Love.

You be the living difference of Joy.

You be the living difference of Peace.

You be the living difference of Patience.

You be the living difference of Kindness.

You be the living difference of Goodness.

You be the living difference of Faithfulness.

You be the living difference of Gentleness.

You be the living difference of Self-control.

The fruit of the Spirit provide life and refreshment, not only to yourself but to those around you. It benefits others—but it starts with you, Mom! What our kids see in us will be reflected in their lives. If you're thinking, *Phew, this is a big job!* you're right. It is a big job. But keep in mind that you're a work in progress too. Every step you take closer to the heart of God will help transform your thinking and actions. It's a lifetime of learning and living it out. Don't give up. You got this!

Even though I'm past the years of rearing my girls and I now find myself contributing to the building up of the next generation, I find myself asking a similar question: What are some qualities you want your (grand)kids to recognize in you? It's a question you too will ask through the different seasons and stages of life. As you think through the qualities you've written down, allow the Holy Spirit to teach you through the Word of God.

> Every step you take closer to the heart of God will help transform your thinking and actions.

I clearly remember years ago, when my girls were in elementary school, I felt like my days were spinning out of control. My to-do list seemed to exceed the allotted twenty-four hours I had each day. Between helping out at the Christian school they attended, holding a neighborhood Bible study in my home, overseeing a children's program at our church, and organizing a newly formed community Bible study, plus managing our home, something had to give. And give, it did.

My relationship with the Lord, that is.

You see, I was doing all these good things for God, but I was missing the most important part of my day: time with Him. I would walk by the chair that once occupied my early morning moments and whisper to God, "I'll be there when ..." Sometimes we can allow the clutter in our lives to overshadow the necessity of living close to God.

When we allow our heart, mind, and soul to be captivated by our time with God, He will reveal the most important next step in our hour, day, month. Let His presence bring order to your thoughts as you set aside alone time with the One who holds your days. Allow His peace to permeate a few minutes of your day to bring wisdom, clarity, and direction. The nearness of God is as close as you make it.

You make time for what is important, don't you?

Many of us have bought into the cultural lie that a busy life is a productive life. And as moms, we thrive on productivity, but it can't be at the expense of our alone time with God. I'm all for a balanced life, and that is what we twenty-first-century women try to achieve, but the one area that should be unbalanced is your time with God. It should be the one thing that tips the teeter-totter to the one side over all the others.

I know the early years of motherhood sometimes seem like they may last forever, but they don't. Eventually the children grow up, and you look back and think it happened in the blink of an eye. We're given only eighteen years, maybe twenty, to rear our children. Trust me when I say that the best thing you can do for your family is to make getting into God's Word a priority. It will be your lifeline!

Look up the following verses and write out the blessings that come from being in God's Word.

Psalm 19:8

Psalm 119:28

Psalm 119:93

Psalm 119:105

Psalm 119:165

God honors and is committed to blessing those who respect and love His precious Word. It is the most valuable possession we own because it's His written message to us. From Genesis to Revelation, God reveals His mind and heart to us. Everything else will pass away, "but the word of our God stands forever" (Isaiah 40:8).

And because your life is transformed as a child of God, Mom, making time to read His Word will affect those around you. You'll begin to treat others the way you want to be treated. It's a ripple effect from God to you and then to others. You won't be perfect and you'll miss the mark at times—we all do!—but it's so worth faithfully pressing on and continuing to walk out this thing we call motherhood.

Maybe you're a mom who works outside the home and you can barely get out the door, but once you do, you have a half-hour commute to work. Or maybe you're a stay-at-home mom who gets some downtime while your children nap. These are the perfect times to listen to a podcast, audiobook, or Christian radio station. Really, it's just about being intentional about doing something—anything—to deepen your relationship with God.

I found that I had to reprioritize and decide what was the most important part of my day, then take steps to keep it that way. Remember, whomever you spend the most time with is who you'll become. So, arise and strive to be the difference in your marriage, your parenting, your relationships, and your daily life. Fixing your eyes on Jesus will change your outlook and attitude.

LET'S HEAR FROM OTHERS

Verna, describing her real-mom solution to staying in the Word when her children were young, says …

After my children were too old for naps, I created a quiet time for them, and that was the time I had mine also, especially if it was interrupted in the early morning. I encourage you women to know that God will honor your efforts in the time you spend with Him, no matter the amount of time, particularly when you're a young and busy mom!

ACTION STEP

Be intentional about meeting with God every day. Commit to reading Psalm 119 this week and note what it says about the importance of being in God's Word. If Psalm 119 is too long, read Psalm 19:7–14 and do the same. (I frequently refer to Psalm 19 as the Cliff Notes for Psalm 119.)

PRAYER

Oh God, You are worthy of all my praise. I thank You that You never leave me nor forsake me. You know my heart's desire to draw closer to You and know You deeper. There are so many areas in my life that vie for my attention, but I know time with You is needed and well spent. So please help me carve out a few minutes each day to be refueled by Your strength and wisdom. You're the source of all I need. Meet me here. Develop in me a love for Your Word and a heart that burns for You. In Your holy name, O God, I pray. Amen.

WRITE OUT YOUR THOUGHTS

THE WISE WOMAN

The wise woman builds her house,
but the foolish tears it down with her own hands.

PROVERBS 14:1

Yesterday we established the importance of being in God's Word, and today we're going to dig a little deeper into ways His Word will increase our wisdom. After all, who doesn't want to gain wisdom?

There are times when I ask God to keep me one step ahead in a particular situation—or with the actions of a three-year-old, ha! Wisdom is wrapped up in the love and commitment of our Savior to guide us along the way. A wise woman turns from the world's beliefs about her to the love of the Father.

As you abide in God's love, you will gain a strength and confidence beyond yourself. His love for you will become a firm foundation to build your days upon, a courage to protect your household, and a strength when things seem to be crumbling around you.

Where or to whom do you turn for advice?

Is the Bible the first or last place you turn to for wisdom?

Look up the following Scripture passages and write down what each one tells you about wisdom and how it encourages you.

Proverbs 1:7

Proverbs 9:9

Proverbs 14:1

James 1:5–6

James 3:17–18

I want to be a wise woman. I want to be a mom who builds her home, not one who tears it down. And I believe you do too. A wise woman desires to walk in the ways of the Lord. She has a healthy fear of God. She is also willing to learn from others and welcomes correction and guidance.

There's a difference between worldly wisdom and biblical wisdom. Today, we can gain all the humanly possible knowledge we can comprehend. Everything is at the touch of a screen. But the wisdom we're talking about is the wisdom that comes from above. Wisdom is more than knowledge; it is also our character. Wisdom is knowing how and when to apply the knowledge we gain. There will be times when godly wisdom won't make sense to a watching world, but when we're acting out of obedience to God, we gain an eternal perspective.

> A wise woman desires to walk in the ways of the Lord. She has a healthy fear of God.

A person can be smart, clever, and insightful, but without character there's an absence of authentic wisdom. This heavenly wisdom is marked with the residue of righteousness. With this in mind, what does a wise person of character look like? They are pure in motive and peace-loving in relationships. They defer to the needs of others, submit to authority, initiate empathy, bear the fruit of the Spirit, gather all the facts before making a decision, and are genuine in their concerns.

What are some ways you can encourage and build the mentioned character qualities in your home?

Write out Proverbs 14:1.

In what ways can a woman build her home?

In what ways can a woman tear down her home?

Let me say this again: You won't get this right all the time. You're a work in progress just like everyone else. But you'll still need to put one foot in front of the other and keep marching on. Oh yes, there will be days you wish you didn't say or do a particular thing, or that you didn't overreact to a situation. There may be times you wish you had a do-over. There will even be days when you don't stay ahead of your toddler and are taken back by his or her actions. But this is what I can tell you: Our God is a God of love and second (and third, and fourth, and ...) chances. He is a God that wants to bestow His wisdom on you.

Because of the hope you have in Christ, He lives in you through His Holy Spirit who guides you each day. He imparts to you the quickening life of Jesus, making you truly alive, and He takes that which was "beyond" you and places it "within" you. Immediately, once "the beyond" has come "within," it rises up to "the above," and you're lifted into the kingdom where Jesus lives and reigns.[1] His personal touch is His Holy Spirit working in you—the "beyond" is brought "within" and takes you to "the above."

At times, we think Jesus is too beyond us and we don't seek Him out, but this couldn't be further from the truth. Jesus is reachable and wants you and me to relentlessly seek Him.

Look up the following Scripture passages. Match the verses with the word that it relates to: Beyond, Within, or Above.

Jeremiah 29:11–14   **Beyond**

Ephesians 3:14–19   **Above**

Philippians 4:10–13   **Within**

He, who at times can feel like He is *beyond* you, is always waiting for you to seek Him. He will allow you to find Him (Jeremiah 29:13), and when you do, He'll make His home *within* you

(Ephesians 3:17) and allow you to live *above* your circumstances with power from on high (Philippians 4:10–13).

Will this type of living take work on your part? Yes! You'll need to be intentional with seeking after Him, but each step will draw you closer to the Father's heart and increase your wisdom.

Is there a difficult situation in your life that's consuming your days? Describe it here.

Do you need a wisdom greater than your own?

Where will you turn for help?

Read Colossians 2:2–3 and write down what is hidden in Christ.

Paul reinforces that wisdom and knowledge are hidden or deposited in Christ alone because the false teachers during his time taught that they're hidden away in mystical experiences and higher knowledge. Christ is all we need! Don't look for treasure that you already have. Christ is our treasure—our gift from God and our fullness of God, so we have been given this fullness. We can treat Him as our treasure, or we can take Him for granted. Paul told the believers about the hidden treasures of wisdom and knowledge because he didn't want them to go on a wild-goose chase. God doesn't want us to be deceived either.

According to 1 Kings 3, King Solomon was told by God that he could ask for anything he wanted and he would receive it. Instead of asking for a long life, riches, popularity, or power, Solomon asked for wisdom. He understood that the "wisdom that comes from above" is the one thing we need more than anything else if we are to be what God wants us to be.

If you were to ask God for one thing, what would it be?

The best thing you can do for your family is to seek the greatest treasure—Jesus. The One who has all the wisdom and knowledge we need to seek.

LET'S HEAR FROM OTHERS

Linda shares,

My two girls were the oldest of four, and they were born eleven months and eleven days apart! There was little time for a quiet time—just a dash to the Upper Room and a quick prayer that often was simply, "Help me, God." My home was built on grabbing hold of one or two verses and tightly holding onto those truths throughout the day. I would pray what I came to call "breath prayers." God knew the growing desire in my heart to know more of Him, His Word, and His wisdom, which He honored through small daily revelations. The more I sought Him, the more He revealed Himself to me.

ACTION STEP

Choose a practical way to build into your home and implement it this week. Encourage a family member. Offer your assistance with something you normally don't assist with. Make a favored meal. Take your kids to church. Read Scripture or pray together. There are so many options.

PRAYER

God, I praise You for the wisdom You bestow on me. I thank You that You're always available for me when I have questions and don't know what to do or how to act. Thank You that I don't have to rely on my own wisdom. Give me grace each day to love my children and see them with Your eyes. Help me to train them diligently. Thank You for the guidance, discernment, and truth Your Spirit provides. In Your holy name, O God, I pray. Amen.

WRITE OUT YOUR THOUGHTS

Day Three

THE CONFIDENT MOM

His pleasure is not in the strength of the horse,
nor his delight in the legs of the warrior; the Lord delights in those
who fear him, who put their hope in his unfailing love.

PSALM 147:10-11 NIV

What a day to remember ...

It was a cold winter day. My girls were in elementary school, and my husband happened to be away for his annual winter camping trip with friends. Early in the morning I was awakened by severe abdominal pain that was so intense that I had to crawl out of my bedroom into the hallway. I gave a faint cry, not wanting to startle my girls but hoping one of them would hear me. Well, it must not have been as faint as I thought, because both girls came running.

They called our neighbor as well as close family friends. Kay took me to the hospital while her husband, Kevin, gathered my girls in their jammies and took them to their home with his own kids in tow. On another day I'll share about the illness I battled during the rearing years of my girls, but this particular hospital visit was due to a residual effect of a medication I was taking.

Although this was a painful situation, God used Kay's and my time together in the emergency room to make a lasting impression on my life—one I will always be grateful for. As you abide in God's love, you will gain a strength and confidence beyond yourself. His love for you will become a firm foundation to build your days upon, a courage to protect your household, and a strength when things seem to be crumbling around you.

To this day, I'm not sure whether Kay fully knows how her words fell fresh on me and changed the trajectory of my days. Yes, they were that impactful! She knew me well and had watched my activity level. She is a wise woman, and I'm sure it wasn't easy for her to verbalize the words she spoke to me. She shared Psalm 147:10–11, "His pleasure is not in the strength of the horse, nor his delight in the legs of the warrior; the Lord delights in those who fear him, who put their hope in his unfailing love" (NIV), and then graciously said, "Jessie, you seem to be working so hard in your own strength, but God wants you to rely on Him."

In such a vulnerable state, I took to heart her observation and agreed with her. I so wanted to be walking in the will of God, but I was getting in front of Him and needed to rely on His strength rather than my own. Maybe you can relate.

Now don't get me wrong, we're to do our work as though we're doing it unto the Lord (see Colossians 3:23–24), but there are many times when we try to do the work in our own power and don't allow God a chance to show His strength.

After that hospital visit over twenty years ago, my days looked different. Are there still days I try to do things in my own strength? You bet. But I'm quickly reminded of that monumental day and I try to redirect my efforts to invite God into the planning.

Write out a monumental conversation or advice that impacted your life.

In what ways do you try to work out of your own strength?

How can you begin to allow God's strength to help guide your day?

Look up the following Scripture passages. Write where confidence is found and how you can apply it to your life.

2 Chronicles 32:7–8

Isaiah 41:10

Acts 4:13

2 Corinthians 3:5–6

It is His adequacy ... His competence ... His confidence that we can tap into. "Whatever your hand finds to do, do it with all your might" (Ecclesiastes 9:10). The message here is that we don't have to stress so much about our own weaknesses. We don't have to be the smartest, the most successful, the most productive, or the most anything. Our job is to do our best and trust that the Lord will work through that.

Jeremiah 17:7–8 gives us the remedy for moving forward despite any inadequacies or doubts that arise: "The man who trusts in the Lord, whose confidence indeed is the Lord, is blessed. He will be like a tree planted by water: it sends its roots out toward a stream, it doesn't fear when heat comes, and its foliage remains green. It will not worry in a year of drought or cease producing fruit" (HCSB).

Expound on the analogy from Jeremiah 17:7–8, "He will be like a tree planted by water..." Put each analogy into your own words and describe how it might manifest in your life.

He will be like a tree planted by water:

it sends its roots out toward a stream,

it doesn't fear when heat comes,

and its foliage remains green.

It will not worry in a year of drought or cease producing fruit.

Jeremiah likens believers to thriving trees planted next to the stream of God's living water. Their roots—which represent their confidence and trust—are sent out to be nourished by the stream, which represents the life found in God. What a beautiful image of flourishing and peace!

Mom, you'll want to drink from the living water each day. Cozy yourself up, read from God's Word, and let it sink into your core so that it'll bring you the needed peace and comfort to help you battle anxiety, stress, and weariness.

It's important to remember that this promise doesn't mean that if we trust in God, we won't have trials and temptations in life. Jeremiah said, "*when* heat comes," not *if*. And Jesus told us in John 16:33, "In the world you will have tribulation" (NKJV).

Nope, there's no getting around troubles and trials. But here's the question: When those trials come, do we want to be all alone in a hot, lifeless desert—or do we want to be rooted next to a flowing stream? If our faith, trust, and confidence is in God, when trials come—and they *will* come—we don't need to be afraid. That's the point Jeremiah was making. Our leaves will remain green, and we will never fail to bear fruit.

When we trust God with our future and find our confidence in Him, He will bless our efforts. This isn't the case when we trust in mere human effort and turn our heart away from Him—that person's life will be cursed (see Jeremiah 17:6). We all need to trust God when our human thoughts want to take us in a different direction.

Put your confidence in God, not man. Your security in Jesus's finished work on the cross will be a strong foundation when all else seems to be crumbling around you. Putting on His armor will give you the strength you need for the situation in front of you.

There's only one way we can stand firm against the trials and even the negative self-talk that bombard our thoughts, and that is by wearing the full armor of God.

Read Ephesians 6:10–18. Describe the pieces of armor we'll need to put on.

We need to understand this spiritual armor in order to best handle our daily battles:

The belt of truth: We accept the truth of the Bible and choose to follow it with integrity. When we do this, we will arm ourselves with truth.

The breastplate of righteousness: In our striving to be Christlike, we live according to His ways of righteousness, which protect our heart. We let our head knowledge of the Scriptures become our breastplate that protects our heart.

Our feet fitted with the readiness: We need to believe the promises of God and count on them to be true. This will keep us steadfast in Christ and standing firm against the lies that come at us.

The shield of faith: This shield will deflect the blows from the swords and arrows of the enemy and help us reject those temptations to doubt and sin. As we build upon our faith daily, we will be shielded by God.

The helmet of salvation: This helmet will help protect our minds. We will need to rest on our trust and hope in the future while living in this world according to the values of heaven.

The sword of the Spirit: This is the Word of the Lord. We'll need to use Scripture specifically in life situations to fend off attacks of the enemy, just as Jesus did when He was tempted by the devil in the wilderness (Matthew 4:1–11).

Put on His full armor and walk in the confidence of Christ. Yes, you can be a woman clothed in strength and dignity and smile at the days ahead (see Proverbs 31:25). For added security, grab a friend and stand back-to-back, both wearing the armor of God, and you'll sense added confidence. Remember, God has kept you alive and given you opportunities for fruitful living.

Paul's impactful words to the Philippians are also for you today, Mom: "For I am confident of this very thing, He who began a good work in you will perfect it until the day of Christ Jesus" (Philippians 1:6).

LET'S HEAR FROM OTHERS

Keri, giving her real-mom solution to being a confident mom, says ...

God's greatest gift to me is my children. As a mom, I taught them about God's love, God's faithfulness, God's mercy, and God's grace. When my toddlers quickly became teenagers, I had to step out of the security of the familiar and find peace in the unfamiliar, praying and trusting God with their lives. I encourage you to put on your armor and teach your children to do the same as you stand firm in God's truth, and to never stop praying for your children!

ACTION STEP

Each morning before you even place your feet on the floor, put on the full armor of God. Think through each piece of armor and what you might need for the day. Battle up, my friend!

PRAYER

Oh Lord, I ask for Your help in remembering to put on Your full armor every day, for You give us all that we need to stand firm in this world. Forgive me, God, for the times I've been unprepared, been too busy to care, or tried to fight and wrestle in my own strength. Thank You that I never fight alone, for You are constantly at work on my behalf, shielding, protecting, strengthening, and covering me from the cruel attacks I face, even when I'm unaware of them. In Your holy name, O God, I pray. Amen.

WRITE OUT YOUR THOUGHTS

Day Four

RESILIENCE IS YOUR SUPERPOWER

No, in all these things we are more
than conquerors through him who loved us.

ROMANS 8:37 NIV

Do you wish you had a superpower like the American comic book heroine Wonder Woman? A woman with superior strength, speed, and agility? A woman who can handle all the things that come her way? Even more, do you ever feel like the world expects you to be Wonder Woman?

Well, you may not be a superhero in a fictitious world, but you can still acquire a superpower beyond your own strength. I truly believe a woman who has accepted the love of God and believes Jesus is our Savior has a superpower—resilience. Resilience comes when God takes a painful circumstance in our life and not only heals us but also makes us even stronger than we were prior to the struggle.

Today, we're going to establish what godly resilience looks like, where we can find it, and how to use it to live out our days.

In your own words, define resilience.

In the following definition, circle the actions or character traits you desire to display.

Resilience: *flexibility, pliability, suppleness, plasticity, elasticity, springiness, durability, ability to last, strength, sturdiness, toughness; strength of character, toughness, hardiness; adaptability, buoyancy, flexibility, ability to bounce back.*[2]

Look up the following Scripture passages about women of valor and match them with the character they possess.

Judges 4:1–9 (Deborah)	**Prioritized her time with the Lord**
Ruth 1:16–18 (Ruth)	**Was determined and committed**
1 Samuel 1:24–28 (Hannah)	**Arose in the face of adversity**
Luke 10:38–42 (Mary)	**Was a woman of prayer**

These are just a handful of women from Scripture who possessed strength that was beyond themselves. They needed a superpower infilling to walk out the destiny of their lives.

In Hebrew, *valor* means to have strength, might, efficiency, wealth, army, ability, efficiency, and force.[3] Often, *valor* is a military term. Oh yes, Mama, many of your days seem like an uphill battle—one that needs strength beyond yourself. You push through, adapt, and pivot. You're stronger than you think! In fact, you're more than a conqueror (see Romans 8:37). The qualities listed above are available to you and me when we turn to the Lord for our strength.

Many of us pray for protection and guidance over our families, and we should. But even so, there are times when difficult situations or heartache invade our life. The women we read about today endured heartache and discouragement too. Deborah had a battle to fight. Ruth lost her husband and homeland. Hannah dedicated her son to the Lord, which in her case meant giving him up for the work of God. Mary was judged by her sister for leaving her work to sit at the feet of Jesus. But each one of these women chose what was right in the eyes of God, and with His strength, she walked out her calling.

What is something God is asking you to do that seems harder than you can accomplish in your own strength?

What valiant character trait will you need to possess to face your situation?

You've probably heard the common saying, "Pull yourself up by your bootstraps." It means to improve your situation by your own efforts—to succeed or elevate yourself without any outside help.[4] At the mention of this gesture, it seems courageous to dig down deep within yourself for needed strength—that is, until your strength isn't enough and the power to withstand something challenging sends you flat on your face.

> No, in all these things we are more than conquerors through Him who loved us.
>
> ROMANS 8:37 NIV

You need more than your own effort to bounce back from heartbreak, stressful situations, or exhaustion. You need something beyond *you*! Specifically, you need God's glorious power working in you. Only then will you be ready for anything, because it's the strength of the One who lives in you that allows you to do all things through Him who strengthens you (see Philippians 4:13).

Write out Philippians 4:13.

This type of strength is only found in Jesus and the power of the Holy Spirit. Don't allow a day to go by without asking for more of the Holy Spirit's power and guidance.

Look up Luke 11:9–13. What does Jesus tell us to ask for more of?

No matter where you find yourself today, something has caused fatigue to grip you in one way or another. Some days are more intense than others, but no matter where you are on the swinging pendulum, you crave a stamina that will carry you through. My friend, it's His power working in you that will provide the resilience you need (see Colossians 1:29). And according to Luke 11:13, you can ask for more of the filling of the Holy Spirit, who will strengthen you.

Hebrews 12:1–2 says, "Therefore, since we have so great a cloud of witnesses surrounding us, let us also lay aside every encumbrance and the sin which so easily entangles us, and let us run with endurance the race that is set before us, fixing our eyes on Jesus, the author and perfecter of faith." To run with endurance, you must first lay aside every burden, such as fear, anxiety, or a hurt-filled past—anything that keeps you from doing what God wants you to do. Second, you must lay aside the sins that entangle you, including those of unbelief, lack of obedience, and any others that continue to hurt God. He wants you to run your race lean and mean, with His endurance fixing your eyes on Jesus.

What might God be asking you to lay aside?

Maybe you're sitting there thinking, *I've done all this, and I still need endurance to run the race set before me.* Hebrews 12:2 continues, "Who for the joy set before Him endured the cross, despising the shame, and has sat down at the right hand of the throne of God." Yes, not all fatigue is from our sin. Some fatigue is the result of going where God says to go and choosing to remain there until God's purpose is fulfilled.

Just as Jesus needed endurance and resilience to accomplish His purpose on earth with the cross, you'll need His endurance and resilience to obey God's calling in your life—motherhood. He's providing that same endurance for you to bravely bear what's in front of you with His power and strength, not your own.

Look up John 4:27–34 and write what food Jesus was filled with.

Doing the will of God was Jesus's fuel to keep going when adversity hit. It wasn't being filled physically, but being filled spiritually, that strengthened Him. The same is true for us—drawing close to Jesus, doing His will, and fulfilling His purpose for our life should override our physical desires and strengthen us for the days ahead.

Scottish teacher and evangelist Oswald Chambers, in his devotional *My Utmost for His Highest*, says, "God does not give us overcoming life; He gives us life as we overcome."[5] Similarly, John 10:10 says, "The thief comes only to steal and kill and destroy; but I [Jesus] came that [you] may have life, and have it abundantly."

No matter what struggle you're experiencing, Jesus can make a way, revive your spirit, and birth new life within you through the Holy Spirit as you lean into Him and His power. Through the process of *overcoming*, you meet Jesus in a deep place of need—a place of full dependence. And through your dependence on Him, you'll develop a quiet sense of security and humble confidence that births a renewed life and resilience beyond yourself, one fully committed to Him.

Put no confidence in your flesh, but have every confidence in the God who made you, called you, saved you, and keeps you. He will accomplish great things through you and provide the resilience you need when you embrace your weakness as His strength and follow His guidance and trust in the promise of His confidence—not yours.

Let's recap:

What is your superpower?

What does godly resilience look like?

Where can you find it and apply it?

LET'S HEAR FROM OTHERS

Lisa's practical explanation is a great analogy for our day on resilience ...

When I think about resilience, the first image that comes to my mind is a rubber band. This image is not as attractive as a scrunchie or a pretty little hair tie. No, I'm picturing one of the big, thick, you-know-it'll-hurt-if-snapped-on-your-skin kind. It is strong. You can stretch it and not wince thinking it's going to break. No, these babies are tough. This is a picture of resilience—elastic, durable, tough, adaptable, and able to bounce back. God has given us everything we need to bounce back from hurts and hard things that hit us in life. You have the same power living inside you that God used to raise Jesus from the dead. We were never intended to live life alone, ill-equipped, or broken. Jesus came that we might have life, and have it to the full. This same resilience described by the image of a rubber band can be found in Jesus.

Lisa continues with a personal application:

My dad had been in and out of the hospital over a period of two years. Each time he had to stay overnight, I was able to stay with him. The night he went to the hospice house,

however, I chose not to stay. The early morning call came with the shocking words "He is gone." The enemy knew where to hit me: "You miss-s-s-s-ed it." I didn't recognize the accusation, the condemnation. Regret hit hard and heavy. I thought, *There's no bouncing back. This can't be fixed. I don't get a redo.* I cried out to the Lord for comfort. In my spirit, I heard His gentle, loving words to me: "Do you think I would let you miss something so important, and then blame you for it?" My eyes were immediately opened to the truth. I recognized my Lord's voice. I found resilience from reading God's Word, which cultivated a listening ear for God's voice. I found resilience to the enemy's lies in God's truth!

God's greatest gift to me is my children. As a mom, I taught them about God's love, God's faithfulness, God's mercy, and God's grace. When my toddlers quickly became teenagers, I had to step out of the security of the familiar and find peace in the unfamiliar, praying and trusting God with their lives. I encourage you to put on your armor and teach your children to do the same as you stand firm in God's truth, and to never stop praying for your children!

ACTION STEP

Today, ask God to give you the strength needed to face what's in front of you. For added encouragement, talk with a close friend about your current situation.

PRAYER

Oh Lord, help me to focus only on today for the strength I need to accomplish what's in front of me. Let me allow the work of Your Spirit to overtake every part of my being so that Your strength will shine through my weakness. I am Yours, and I want to be pliable in Your capable hands. Help me to be aware when I try to do things in my own strength. I desire Your power, Your perseverance, and Your pliancy. In Your holy name, O God, I pray. Amen.

WRITE OUT YOUR THOUGHTS

Day Five

PERFECTION VS. EXCELLENCE

Strength and dignity are her clothing,
and she smiles at the future.

PROVERBS 31:25

Do you, at times, feel like you're called to be perfect? Perfect in every area of your life?
The perfect height?
The perfect weight?
The perfect attitude?
The perfect home?
The perfect relationship?
The perfect mom?

Do you bring the attitude of perfection on yourself, or do you allow others to heap it upon you?

What is the driving force behind perfectionism?

If you find yourself struggling with perfectionism, you'll need to get a handle on it or you'll end up passing it down to your children, because you'll apply perfectionistic standards to not only yourself, but also to the people around you.

And although you may appear successful to others, there are probably times when you feel you aren't enough. You don't measure up to the other moms. You always feel like you need to be strong and "in control" of your emotions, and that admitting your weaknesses or asking for help isn't acceptable because people will think less of you. Sometimes, putting the pressure on yourself to be perfect and live a Pinterest-worthy life will even stop you from moving forward out of fear that you won't do it well enough.

Can you relate?

One of the greatest freedoms I found while raising my girls came when I no longer allowed other moms to place their convictions on me. By convictions, I mean their personal preferences, not godly beliefs.

You are unique. It may cause difficulties in a friendship because you don't act or do things exactly like your friend. Your child may have a bent toward athletics while your friend's child is more musical. Her daughter may like to wear dresses while your daughter likes to sport sweatpants and jeans. Your son may like to wrestle while your friend's son prefers to sit quietly and play by himself. Bottom line, you'll need to decide what's best for you and your family and not try to fit into someone else's mold of who they think you should be.

> What you believe at your core is going to dictate your actions. Where you find your worth will drive your steps, your living, and your parenting style.

Do you find yourself trying to fit into someone else's mold of who they think you should be? If yes, what will you need to do to reverse this thought pattern?

Hopefully, you and your friend are able to accept each other's differences and move past unnecessary expectations. But if not, the friendship may have been only for a season. Handle it with grace and move on. Don't feel like you have to fulfill someone else's purpose. There's a fine line between perfection and a healthy pursuit of excellence.

Write out your definition of perfection.

Write out your definition of excellence.

Perfectionism comes from external comparison, whereas excellence is the satisfaction of achievement that comes from within, no matter what you've done.[6] Perfectionism is focused on "doing the thing 'right,'" how things appear, and whether others think it's done right. Excellence is about "doing the right thing." It's focused on the reason for a task, and the results for it to be a success.[7] What you believe at your core is going to dictate your actions. Where you find your worth will drive your steps, your living, and your parenting style.

Look up the following Scripture passages and write what each verse says about your worth.

Psalm 17:8

Psalm 139:17–18

Colossians 3:12

1 Peter 2:9

When you come to the monumental realization that you're loved and cherished by God, nothing others say about you will affect your actions. Oh boy, don't you wish that statement was true? Yes, we still may be hurt by others' statements or allegations and may be impacted by their choices—but we don't have to allow the words people say to stick to us. That's why it's important to believe what God says about us and not what the world says—or what that pesky, judgmental voice inside us whispers.

The Bible provides us with a positive woman we can look to with great admiration and view as an example of right living. Some may say, "There's no way one woman can be all that. None of us can be perfect." That's true, but I say we can still aspire to be the Proverbs 31 woman. She is a woman who strives for excellence in every area of her life.

Being a Proverbs 31 woman is not about being perfect. It's about living life with purpose and excellence. My dear friend Sally once told me, "The Proverbs 31 woman is not about how much she is doing, but about what and why she is doing the doing." The Proverbs 31 woman lives a very intentional life. I don't bring her up to make you and me feel less than adequate, but to provide an example we can strive toward. She's a woman we can aspire to be.

I know, I know. You may have read Proverbs 31 many times in the past, but please don't skip over this reading and exercise. I pray something new and refreshing will speak to you today.

Read Proverbs 31:10–31. Write down the characteristics and the corresponding verse that make up the Proverbs 31 woman. (I'll help you get started.)

Trustworthy (v. 11)

What characteristic(s) do you excel at?

What characteristic(s) do you need to work on?

The Proverbs 31 woman is brave, is faithful; is a planner; works with vigor; takes care of herself and her family; and is hospitable, observant, diligent, and encouraging. She manages and guards her household, all while fearing the Lord. But the most important aspect of this virtuous woman is her spiritual life. She is a godly woman who fears the Lord (Proverbs 31:30).

This proverb is a twenty-two-line, alphabetic Hebrew poem not only about our role as a woman, but about the character that transcends both gender and circumstance. The author is essentially showing us what wisdom looks like in action—"a virtuous woman who can find?" is best translated "a woman of valor who can find?" As a reminder from yesterday's reading, in the Hebrew, a woman of valor (*chayil*)[8] means a woman of strength, might, ability, efficiency, wealth, army. Think of it as "You go, girl!"

A woman of valor is powerful because of her relationship with her Creator. This doesn't mean that she's powerful in her own strength. To be the Proverbs 31 woman, you'll need to reach deep within and rely on the power of the Holy Spirit.

So, how do we move from perfectionism to striving for excellence?

- Humble yourself before the Lord (see James 4:10).
- Abandon comparison (see 2 Corinthians 10:12).
- Get busy serving the Lord, using the gifts He has gifted you with (see Luke 4:8).
- Pursue righteousness (see Proverbs 21:21).
- Ask God for wisdom (see James 1:5).
- Commit to the task at hand, not the results (see Psalm 37:5).
- Rest in God's grace, knowing that in His sovereignty, He redeems all things (see 2 Corinthians 12:9).

Mom, the highest praise—and the deepest freedom—belongs to the woman who chooses to pursue excellence over perfectionism in her calling. "Many women do noble things, but you surpass them all" (Proverbs 31:29 NIV). When you read about the Proverbs 31 woman, do you think of her as Superwoman? Do you get burned out just reading about all her accomplishments?

Yes, there is sacrifice, discipline, and diligence that comes along with aspiring to the role of this woman. But let me encourage you, this portion of Scripture was not a snapshot of her twenty-four-hour day, but of her life. I believe this is a conglomerate of the seasons of her life, and if you fix your eyes on Jesus, the author and perfecter of your faith, you will not grow weary and lose heart (see Hebrews 12:2–3). He will give you the strength to wake up early, serve your family with joy, work with your hands and not be idle, and extend your hand to the needy.

As I continued to read through Proverbs 31, I noticed that in the twenty-two verses, the word *household* is mentioned four times.

PROVERBS 31:15
"She rises also while it is still night and gives food to her *household*."

PROVERBS 31:21
"She is not afraid of the snow for her *household*, for all her *household* are clothed with scarlet."

PROVERBS 31:27
"She looks well to the ways of her *household*, and does not eat the bread of idleness."

If *household* is mentioned this frequently, it must be of great importance. This indicates the attention a woman of valor gives to her home should be a priority. No matter whether you work in the home or outside of it, prioritizing your family and home will be a reflection of your relationship with God. Your home is a place of refuge and safety for your family. A place we desire to bring a taste of heaven to earth.

I know, I know. Home isn't always the Pinterest-perfect place displayed in a lot of people's highlight reels, but it can still be our goal to make it a place our friends and family want to come to. Clean or messy, it's still inviting. The feeling of home can be a sweet sentiment to all who enter through our doors.

What will you do today to make your home a place of importance?

Mama, you can live out the Proverb 31 woman's life with excellence as you purposefully pursue God's plan for you.

Phew. Great job. You've now completed the first week of *Mama, You Be the Difference*. You're off to a great start! Keep it up!

LET'S HEAR FROM OTHERS

Sue beautifully shares ...

As a young mom, I was exasperated by the Proverbs 31 woman. She is described as the ideal portrait of biblical womanhood, and the "personification of wisdom" (even though I bet she was always exhausted). She was a gal who seemed to have it all together. She has always intrigued me, and I must confess, I've probably resented her once or twice. I've wondered what her name was, or if she was cranky before her morning coffee. Did she ever bounce a check, or hide candy bars in her closet so her kids couldn't find them? What I really want to know is how she had the time to sew garments, when I struggle to find the time to floss.

Secretly, I'm not sure we could have been friends. But, as the years have passed, I've grown to understand her a lot more, and why God shared this passage with us. She isn't in the Bible to scorn us, but to mentor us. So much can be gleaned from reflecting, and applying her wisdom and character.

We know from Scripture that Jesus Christ was the only perfect, sinless one to roam this earth. Now I'm not rejoicing because the Proverbs 31 gal wasn't perfect, but she wasn't perfect! This means that she was an imperfect woman who served *excellently*. I've also come to understand that this gal wasn't caught up in the comparison game. How do I know? One could argue that she was too busy to be concerned with what others were doing or how they were doing it. But the truth is, she was clothed in dignity and strength (v. 25) and she spoke with wisdom (v. 26).

ACTION STEP

Memorize Psalm 139:17–18: "How precious are your thoughts about me, O God. They cannot be numbered! I can't even count them; they outnumber the grains of sand! And when I wake up, you are still with me!" (NLT).

PRAYER

Oh Lord, You know I want to do things perfectly at times. What You want most is for me to rest in Your presence so I'll know the next steps to take. Please forgive me when I try to take control of all situations and leave You out of the equation. Help me trust You with my insecurities and faults, so that I will find strength in You rather than relying on myself to figure it all out. In Your holy name, O God, I pray. Amen.

WRITE OUT YOUR THOUGHTS

WEEK TWO

Sometimes, we can allow
the clutter in our lives
to overshadow the necessity
of living close to God.

JESSIE SENECA

THE CONNECTION

"Abide in me, and I in you. As the branch cannot bear fruit by itself,
unless it abides in the vine, neither can you, unless you abide in me.
I am the vine; you are the branches. Whoever abides in me and I in him,
he it is that bears much fruit, for apart from me you can do nothing."

JOHN 15:4–5 ESV

This week we're going to dive into the meaning of connection. Connection to an amazing God and connection to people. Too many times we can get caught up in things rather than relationships. I don't believe we intentionally set out to accumulate "stuff" or make our possessions our god. However, it seems that once the little ones come along, stuff starts to pile up and we find ourselves buried beneath more than we signed up for.

Recently, I had the tough job of cleaning out my mom's home and then shortly after that helping pack up my in-law's home of nearly fifty years to move them into an apartment a mile and a half from our home. These two tasks helped put life into perspective. Life really does boil down to this: love God and love others. Stuff will come and go and really doesn't satisfy in the end, but true satisfaction comes when your fulfillment comes from pleasing God.

Look up Matthew 22:36–40 and write out the commands of God.

The common denominator to both commands is love. We need to allow love to rule our thoughts, actions, and motives. This isn't always easy though, is it? There will be days when you love your child but you may not like them. One of my daughters once asked me, "Is it possible to have a favored child?" I chuckled and responded, "Yes, it's possible, but that child will change with different seasons of parenting." Even so, through it all, if you love your children in view of eternity, it will change the way you see them and the way you parent.

When our connection vertically to God is intact, our connection horizontally with others will be better.

So, let's start with our connection to God.

Look up John 15:1–9 and write what these verses say about whom or what we should abide (remain) in.

One of my favorite chapters in the Bible is John 15. Many times, it's my go-to read. *Abide* means to remain, dwell, continue, tarry, and endure.[9] We are to enjoy our time in God's presence and not rush through it as another task. Pull up a chair and stay for a while with Jesus. Commune with Him before others and listen to His voice through the reading of His Word. Some days it may be reading and reflecting on only one verse, and other days it may be a half hour of reading. The most important thing is that you're turning to God's Word for guidance.

> "I am the vine, you are the branches; he who abides in Me and I in him, he bears much fruit, for apart from Me you can do nothing."
>
> JOHN 15:5

John 15 describes our connection to Jesus as a branch connected to the vine—and a branch cannot bear fruit without the vine. If you pluck a luscious bunch of grapes from a vine, you could eat them. But leave them on the counter or in the sun, and eventually they'll rot or shrivel up. Only fruit connected to the plant will grow, thrive, and bear more fruit. It must be connected to the vine to be healthy and fruitful.

It's the same with us. We must stay connected to the vine (Jesus), our main source of strength. It's not the branch that produces the fruit, but the vine to which the branch is connected. When we stay connected to Jesus, we can endure. If we try to do it alone, we'll dry up just as the grapes do when they're off the vine.

Mama, let your main source of strength be your connection to the giver of life—Jesus. Will there still be some days that are just plain hard? Yes. But if you're connected to Jesus, you'll be able to walk through them a little more focused, stronger, and at peace.

Continue reading John 15:11–16 and match the verse with the action that accompanies abiding.

John 15:11	**Enjoy friendship with Jesus**
John 15:13	**Experience joy**
John 15:14	**Lay down your life for others**
John 15:15	**Bear much fruit**
John 15:16	**Increase in wisdom from God**

As you and I abide with Jesus, it will require greater actions from us. Dwelling in His presence should not only impact our hearts, but also our actions and conduct, and it will bring glory to God. There will be days when, amid living out your motherhood calling, you'll be required to lay your life down for your family—that's called sacrifice. Some days you'll need wisdom beyond your own knowledge. Other days you'll need joy that will override your circumstances. All of this is found only in your connection to Jesus.

I know today's reading includes a lot of Scripture to look up, but I also know it will enrich your life. John delves deeper into the meaning of abiding and the effects it should have on our lives. In 1 John, the word *abide* appears over twenty times, making it a vital focus of his teaching.

Look up the following verses in 1 John and write down the effect that accompanies abiding. (I'll help get you started with the first effect.)

1 John 2:6
When we abide in Christ, we will walk (live) in the same manner as Jesus.

1 John 2:10

1 John 2:24–25

1 John 2:27

1 John 2:28

1 John 3:17–18

The more connected you remain to Jesus, the more you'll be able to walk out these actions. The practice of abiding is a lifetime commitment to seeking God and experiencing His presence. The more you abide in Him, the more He'll expose Himself to you. Where you position God will be how He relates to you. The God of the universe invites all of us into an up-close-and-personal relationship.

What part of your day might you need to change to be more connected to Jesus and find time to abide in Him?

LET'S HEAR FROM OTHERS

Tabitha shares ...

Connect with God first to connect with others best. The time you set aside to simply abide will not only replenish your supply, but will also allow you to meet the needs of your family from a place of rest, not stress. Being a child of God and a student of His Word makes us a better mom to our kids and equips us to teach them His ways as well. When we connect with God daily, He'll give us what we need to connect with our kids consistently and continually.

I'm a morning person, so as soon as my feet hit the floor, my coffee is poured and my Bible is open. When my kids wake up, instead of closing my Bible, I invite them to join me in conversation over what I just read and studied. Those conversations keep our hearts connected throughout the day, no matter where we are, in the kitchen or in the car.

ACTION STEP

Spend concentrated time with God reading John 15. Add an extra five minutes to your time if needed.

PRAYER

Oh Lord, I thank You that You never move. You are always waiting for me with open arms. You're faithful when I have been unfaithful. Forgive me for the times I haven't prioritized my time with You and have allowed other things and relationships to take Your place. You know my desire is to draw close to You. Please keep me in the palm of Your hand and guide me in my everyday life. In Your holy name, O God, I pray. Amen.

WRITE OUT YOUR THOUGHTS

Day Two

SISTERING

*Sweet friendships refresh the soul and awaken our hearts with joy, for good friends
are like the anointing oil that yields the fragrant incense of God's presence.*

PROVERBS 27:9 TPT

Yesterday we spent some time looking at our connection to God and how that connection nourishes our relationship with others. Over the next few days, we'll look at the necessity of having other women in our life and how we foster those relationships to the fundamental importance of like-minded people in our children's lives.

What comes to your mind when you read the word *sistering*?

A dear friend of mine, Linda, defines sistering like this: "Sistering is two women coming together to share their hearts and lives, and when they depart from their time together each one believes they were the one who got the greatest blessing."

Sisterhood, done right, can be one of the best parts of our lives as women. We want these relationships. We long for these relationships. We need these relationships.

The suffix -*ing*, defined by Merriam-Webster, denotes a verbal action relating to an occupation or skill.[10] So sister*ing* would mean a woman or girl in relation to other daughters and sons of her parents, or a close female friend or associate, acting out her role. With this in mind, sister*ing* is an action verb.

It's part of our DNA to cultivate lasting relationships with other women. Even though we experience hurtful situations at times, we still desire them because we're meant to build into each other's lives. We're meant for relationships, not isolation.

In my book *Friendship Sisters for a Journey*, I used this term and dedicated a whole chapter to *Sistering*. After writing that chapter and then offering a conference on friendship, a woman came up to me and asked, "Did you know sistering is a carpentry term too?"

No, I didn't.

You know it. I went right home and started researching and found the parallel riveting. When you sister a beam, floor joint, or pillar, you add extra material to strengthen damaged material. You normally can't remove the damaged beam, so you add strength to the existing beam on either side. Just as with a damaged beam, when you're hurting, you surround yourself with strong women on either side who will strengthen and support you for what lies ahead.

Share a story from your life that shows sistering in action.

Look up Ecclesiastes 4:9–12 and write out the aspects of sistering you see in this passage.

> A person standing alone can be attacked and defeated, but two can stand back-to-back and conquer. Three are even better, for a triple-braided cord is not easily broken.
>
> ECCLESIASTES 4:12

As you look at Ecclesiastes 4:9–12 and the armor of God (Ephesians 6:10–18) from "The Confident Mom" (day three of week one), you'll see that when two believers come together with the full armor of God on and are standing back-to-back, they can conquer whatever is in front of them with more strength and focus. They will be completely covered on all sides, even their backs.

But the most important piece of the armor is prayer: "With all prayer and petition pray at all times in the Spirit" (Ephesians 6:18). If you have a faithful praying sister upholding you, you're a fortunate, blessed girl. Prayer is the catalyst for a strong friendship, so you must allow others to join you.

Uphold you.

Carry you.

Encourage you.

And sometimes drag you.

This is *sistering* at its best.

What are some qualities you value in your friendships? What qualities do you want to emulate?

Throughout Scripture we read about important friendships that will be a guide for us—from Ruth and Naomi, Elijah and Elisha, and David and Jonathan, to the New Testament friendship between Paul and Timothy.

Look up the following Scripture passages. Write out the names of the people involved in these friendships and the qualities of the relationships.

Ruth 1:14–18

1 Samuel 18:1–4

2 Kings 2:1–11

1 Timothy 1:1–5

I'd like to expound on David and Jonathan's friendship—a true friendship with a special bond. Initially, David was liked by Saul, the king chosen by the people. Saul brought David into the palace to help soothe him by playing his harp. But with David's rising popularity among the people, Saul became jealous of David after his victory over Goliath. Their relationship changed due to the green-eyed monster of jealousy and resentment. But David was strengthened by the personal affection of Jonathan, Saul's oldest son and heir to the throne. Jonathan knew God's favor was upon David, the king chosen by God.

Later on, in 1 Samuel, we see David and Jonathan's friendship bond through empowerment and applause:

> Now David became aware that Saul had come out to seek his life while David was
> in the wilderness of Ziph at Horesh. And Jonathan, Saul's son, arose and went to
> David at Horesh, and encouraged him in God. Thus he said to him, "Do not be afraid,
> because the hand of Saul my father will not find you, and you will be king over Israel
> and I will be next to you; and Saul my father knows that also." So the two of them

made a covenant before the Lord; and David stayed at Horesh while Jonathan went to his house. (1 Samuel 23:15–18)

Much can happen during a wilderness experience. We've all had them. An inhospitable event, situation, or, yes, even friendship. But what I'd like to focus on is a forever friendship. A friendship that weathers the wilderness times, the moments of despair, the days of remorse, and, equally as important, the successes of life.

In the wilderness of Horesh, we see Jonathan loved his friend with deep care when he could have despised him. He encouraged David to stay strong in his faith in God and to not be afraid. They made a covenant, an agreement, before God and with each other to take care of one another. Such warm sympathy, such glowing trustful words, you may well imagine, raised the spirits of David and gave him new courage to face the grave difficulties ahead of him.

That is the type of friend I desire to be.

Encouraging.

Strengthening.

Sympathetic.

God-fearing.

We might never get it all right, but it sure is worth the effort. Even if we try to be one of these to someone in the day before us, we will feel that we've accomplished great things.

Have you had the privilege to have this type of David and Jonathan friendship? If yes, share how you met your friend and how your life was impacted.

This type of friendship can be few and far between and may not have entered your life yet. That's okay. Be grateful for the friendships you have, and appreciate the women in your life at this stage of motherhood. There are seasons of friendship.

American investment banker, financier, and author Ziad Abdelnour tells us, "There are three types of friends: friends for a reason, friends for a season and friends for a lifetime."[11] Some friends are with us for a reason (a specific goal or purpose from God). Some friends are with us for a season (a particular time in His plan). Very few will walk beside us as our forever friend.

The only true friend we must walk with for a lifetime is Jesus. As we do, we can trust He'll bring friends alongside us for a reason, season, or lifetime in the ways and times that are truly best.

Tomorrow, we'll continue to look at the importance of friendships and the benefits of having other role models in our children's lives.

LET'S HEAR FROM OTHERS

Tami shares ...

In midlife I went through a difficult season when I felt unmoored by events I couldn't understand or make sense of. It was a classic existential faith crisis, or, as some call it today, a kind of deconstructing. My two best friends reacted very differently to me during this time. One friend distanced herself completely, and this was deeply painful. My other friend was not afraid to listen to my questions and doubts. She didn't judge or criticize but kept asking good questions and prayed for me. She was steady, faithful, and committed. Even when I was likely a real pain to listen to. My faith eventually regained strength and has become stronger than it was before—by God's grace and my forever friend's prayers (and patience)! I thank God for her often, and learned a lot about how to be a friend to someone in hard places. Yes, this is *sistering* at its best.

ACTION STEP

For the next week, on a separate piece of paper or in your workbook, keep a "grateful" list. Each day write out something or someone you're grateful for and why.

PRAYER

Oh Lord, thank You for the friendships You have brought into my life and the impact they have made on my character. Help me be a good friend to those I do life with. May I represent You in ways that inspire them to be a better version of themselves and be an encouragement to them. May our friendships be a reflection of You. In Your holy name, O God, I pray. Amen.

WRITE OUT YOUR THOUGHTS

Day Three

IT TAKES A VILLAGE

[PART ONE]

Show family affection to one another with brotherly love.

Outdo one another in showing honor.

ROMANS 12:10 HCSB

I would like to take the better part of this day to share with you my story and the importance of others in your life and the lives of your children.

In the summer of 1992, I was twenty-seven years old and a young mom of two girls, two-and-a-half-year-old Lauren and four-month-old Sarah. During these days, which included many fun activities, my life began to change. It seemed as though my family hit one detour after the next.

I was frustrated by the onset of acne on my face, arms, and back. Then my hands started to tremble and I was more anxious than usual. My face became puffy, making me look like I'd just had my wisdom teeth removed. I dismissed these as "normal mom things" due to stress. Potty training a two-year-old. Nursing an infant. And trying to have dinner on the table on time. You can relate, right?

But with each passing month, things progressed from bad to worse and I grew more discouraged. Since I had never really been sick before this time and had only been hospitalized when my girls were born, I really didn't know where to begin.

Finally, I went to my primary care physician. He treated me with antidepressants for anxiety, but I wasn't satisfied with the outcome of that visit. My frustration continued to build.

A few months passed, and Thanksgiving arrived. I had the entire meal prepared, but was unable to serve it due to a severe anxiety attack. My sister-in-law was gracious enough to come and retrieve all the food and our girls, and take them to her house to host the meal for twenty-plus family members. Feeling as though my world was closing in, and with little reprieve from the antidepressant medicine, I ended up in the emergency room of a local hospital.

> And coming to Him as to a living stone which has been rejected by men, but is choice and precious in the sight of God, you also, as living stones, are being built up as a spiritual house for a holy priesthood, to offer up spiritual sacrifices acceptable to God through Jesus Christ.
>
> 1 PETER 2:4–5

Shortly after that ER visit, things spiraled downward even farther. My anxiety hit its peak, and feeling as though I couldn't properly care for my girls anymore, I made my first trip, at my in-laws' coaxing, to the same hospital's psychiatric floor on the day of my brother's birthday. What a present.

I spent that Christmas entrapped in what felt like a prison to me. I was away from my family, in a lonely place, and unaware of what lay ahead, but very much aware of the dark hours of the present day.

And then came some answers. The doctors had determined I had Cushing's syndrome, a rare endocrine disorder that occurs when the adrenal glands release too much of the hormone cortisol into the body. Most Cushing's tumors are located on the pituitary gland, but they can present themselves anywhere else in the body too, most likely in the lungs, adrenal glands, or bronchial tubes. Due to the excess amount of cortisol, many physical and mental problems can occur, which I experienced during the months ahead.

My Christmas hospital stay began a five-month in-patient journey at four different facilities, from December through Easter of the following year. Just a few days after New Year's Eve, I was transported to a city hospital, where they performed pituitary surgery to correct the disease. Just days after the surgery, the psychiatric department and the neurosurgeon fought over my release. (Months later we were informed that this first surgery was unnecessary, as there was never a tumor on my pituitary.)

The third hospital was a second psychiatric facility, which became my home for two and a half months. While hospitalized at this facility, my mental state continued to plummet, my physical symptoms continued to worsen, and I was deteriorating at an alarming rate.

Along with the acne, increased anxiety, and depression, I developed hair growth on my face, a hump on my upper back, diabetes mellitus, loss of bladder control, and weight gain around my middle. Plus my will to live was gone. The doctors seemed to be treating only the mental part of the disease, having me take four different tranquilizers that should have never been taken together.

And then there was a break in my journey. My husband, John, received a note from a neighbor who knew a friend of a friend who'd battled Cushing's. She gave him the name of a doctor in Virginia who had treated her for the same disease. Upon hearing my story, the doctor told John, "You need to bring her down here—like yesterday!"

After a difficult discharge from the psychiatric hospital in Pennsylvania, my husband, my brother, and I took a five-hour road trip to the University of Virginia Hospital. And a road trip it was!

Once I was admitted, the doctors knew what was wrong just by looking at me. Still, they did extensive testing and retesting to confirm their suspicions. The results pointed to an ectopic tumor on my left lung, and they immediately scheduled surgery to remove it. This time the surgery was successful, but the thought of being reunited with my family brought waves of emotions I didn't anticipate. Fear, doubt, and uncertainty became my traveling companions. Seeing my girls only two times in the last five months had caused me to feel less than adequate and wonder, *Will they even remember me?*

Sarah, who was now close to eleven months old, welcomed me home by walking up to me and saying, "Mama." Lauren, whose third birthday was just around the corner, was excited for Mommy to be back home and greeted me with a big hug. All my reservations were wiped away with a hug and a kiss, and with the passing of each day, things started to return to normal.

Even so, the disease brought another three lung surgeries, with the third being the removal of my left lung. Another tumor was found in my chest cavity, and that was removed too. Plus a tubal ligation at the age of twenty-seven was hard to accept.

Now, fast-forward more than twenty years to today. Thankfully, I have been free of the disease for thirteen years. One prayer I always prayed as my girls were growing up was, "Lord, let me live long enough to raise my girls." And here I am enjoying being a mimi. I don't take one day for granted and am so thankful to be writing this study. What a gift!

I share this story with you to say, God has a plan. Sometimes the ways our lives play out aren't how we planned it, but if we can be the best learners we can be through it all, God will use our difficulties and grow us to be more like Him. I wholeheartedly believe He knows what it will take for us to be more like Him—and if it's through heartache, hold on and allow Him to walk through it with you.

Look up Isaiah 45:2–3 and write out what you find in the secret place with God.

Yes, you and I can discover many treasures in dark places if we look for them. One of the greatest treasures I received through the years of battling an illness was the importance of friends, not only in my life but in the lives of my girls. It takes a village to raise children.

Your "village" has never been more necessary than it is today. We live in a fast-paced, instant-information, pressure-packed world, and today's children are faced with a myriad of challenges, opportunities, and temptations. Navigating parenthood can be a daunting undertaking whether we're married or single. Partnerships and support should be welcome and necessary to prepare your children for tomorrow.[12]

Look up the following passages and write out who is involved and what each verse says about the importance of influence and what actions we should take in the role of supporting each other.

John 15:13

Ephesians 6:1–4

2 Timothy 1:5

Titus 2:3–5

Notice in 2 Timothy 1:5, Timothy's grandmother and mother both shared their faith, making Timothy a third-generation Christian. His faith in Christ was genuine and sincere. He honestly trusted Christ as his Savior and Lord, and he lived for Him day by day.

One of the major reasons for his strength in the Lord was the strong and sincere faith of his mother, Eunice, and his grandmother, Lois. They had rooted and grounded him in the faith as seen further in 2 Timothy 3:15: "From childhood you have known the sacred writings which are able to give you the wisdom that leads to salvation through faith which is in Christ Jesus."

Did you have godly influences in your life when you were growing up?
If yes, share one of those influences.

If not, it can start with you! What will you do to make this an important part of raising your kids?

One of my greatest joys has been becoming a mimi. Never did I think my heart could expand and explode in the ways it has. Yes, raising my girls was a high (with a few lows thrown in over the years—ha). But getting a second chance at parenting has been a delight. Of course, I'm not the main caregiver but a contributor. Talk about perspective. When you get a redo, you see things from a totally different angle. Grandparenting has been such a joy, and I wouldn't exchange it for the world!

Write down the names of the people in your life who contribute to the building up of your children, both family and friends.

As your children grow and enter school age, they will be influenced by people outside your controlled nucleus, such as schoolteachers, Sunday school teachers, youth group leaders, coaches, and other children and their parents. Building a firm foundation in their formative years will help them stand firm when trials and temptations persuade them. While they won't always make the right decision, you will be there to help them through the process.

My family was so very thankful for the like-minded community of friends we had around us while the girls were growing up. They were friends who we spent endless hours with, from Friday-night pizza dinners, to church activities, to school projects, to vacations. Intentionally building community is a critical part of raising your children.

Look up 1 Peter 2:4–5 and write down who represents the living stones.

You and your friends are like living stones. Each one of you portrays a stone that makes up a spiritual temple. You are becoming more like Jesus, the Living Stone. You're continually conformed into His image as you seek Him, being built into a spiritual house—durable, living, and active. This is a process you and your friends will continue to build upon. One stone is not a temple. You're a community with many stones building into your family's lives.

Having like-minded people in your children's lives is so important, as there will be times when your kids will listen to them better than they'll listen to you. And if you and your friends are on the same page, you'll have the security of trusting they will give good advice.

LET'S HEAR FROM OTHERS

My daughter Lauren wrote this to a dear friend in our family's life, Sarah, when this friend celebrated her sixtieth birthday (there's more about Sarah in the next chapter) ...

Big Sarah, the one who just happens to be the "older" Sarah and got stuck with a less-than-favorable name that we know you've come to love—today is about celebrating you and the gift you are in our lives. Thank you for helping raise me and Sarah—for all the dinners, loads of laundry, and wisdom you instilled in us. Your love, sacrifice, prayers, and consistent presence throughout our lives has had a bigger impact than you'll ever know. You even came to Grandparents' Day with us so that Sarah and I each had someone with whom to share in the day. We love you very, very much. And although life has begun to look different as the years progress, your influence and love are always with me.

ACTION STEP

Consider an action you can take that will be a help to a friend and implement it. Put action to your good intentions.

PRAYER

Dear Lord, thank You for the people You have brought into my life. Those who have contributed to my and my children's lives. Help me slow down enough to be grateful and show my appreciation to them. There are times I've taken my family and friends for granted, and for that I am sorry. I want to represent You well and live out our friendship in a tangible way—a way that says thank you. Show me how to do this and to be intentional with each relationship. In Your holy name, O God, I pray. Amen.

WRITE OUT YOUR THOUGHTS

Day Four

IT TAKES A VILLAGE

[PART TWO]

A friend loves at all times,
and a brother is born for a difficult time.

PROVERBS 17:17 HCSB

As I was writing about the importance of others in our lives and the lives of our children, one of my closest friends sent a text to me and my daughters that said, "Saw this today and thought of us! Love you all!" It was a Facebook post about being a bonus mom, titled "To my friend's kids."

Before we explore being a bonus mom tomorrow, I want to first address the text from my friend. She said "thought of us," not "thought of you." That little phrase, "thought of us," is what sistering is all about: love, selflessness, care, and inclusion. What would we do without our friends?

On the morning of my lung removal, I wrote a poem, "My Forever Friend." The night before, it had taken me a while to fall asleep. Well, if you can call it that. I drifted off and then the tossing and turning began. Off and on, opening my eyes and shutting them. Sometimes sleeping for minutes and sometimes a half hour.

Needless to say, it was a long night, and I suspect you've had these kinds of nights too!

When I no longer could fall back asleep in the dark, early hours of the morning, I arose and went into the hotel bathroom so I wouldn't bother John. Soon I was on the bathroom floor praying, crying, and praying some more.

Then it happened. Although it had never happened before (and never after), God spoke a poem into my heart for a dear friend. I retrieved the hotel pen and lined note paper and the words began to flow. I'm not sure it was ever meant to be print quality, but it was from my heart back to God's ears, and I hope it will bless you.

My Forever Friend

JESSIE SENECA

I often wish God blessed me long ago
through the years of hopes and dreams,
but He waited till this season of my life
for our friendship, it seems.

Some friends come and some friends go,
and others we may never know,
but friends like you are a gift
wrapped with a heavenly bow.

You're always there with a word
to turn our eyes upon the Lord;
with keeping on your knees,
God is always pleased.

Friends may last a day,
and some friends through tomorrow,
then God gives us friends like you
who are there through and through.

I enjoy our late-night desires,
sipping tea by the fire,
bringing up new conversation,
and working through old frustrations.

Your love and care
are always there
through the joys and sorrows;
you are continually there to uplift my tomorrows.

Things will come and Things will go,
And Things will not matter, we know,
but in the end, it is the love we show
with God's glorifying glow.

A friend like you
I would never want to replace
because of the joys you bring in big and small ways;
it makes you my friend forever and always.

God uses all types and styles of friendships to make us more like Him!

In the first week of this study, we read about the importance of our relationship with God. Yes, enjoying our relationship with Him will be the basis of all other friendships, but we also need God with skin on.

Look up Acts 4:36–37 and note the term given to Barnabas.

The apostles *called* him Barnabas. Barnabas was not his birth name but his given name.

Barnabas = Encourager.

Why? Well, we see him living out his internal belief system and love for God's work when Scripture tells us he sold his land and gave the money to the apostles. Barnabas was a friend to all the apostles, but one stood out in particular—Paul.

After Paul's conversion on the road to Damascus (Acts 9), Paul went to Arabia for three years (Galatians 1:15–18). When he returned to Jerusalem, the disciples were afraid to associate with him, only remembering who he had previously been—Saul, the persecutor of the Christian church. Barnabas, however, was willing to accept Paul as a friend and student (Acts 9:26–30).

He took Paul, who was completely disconnected from the other apostles, and persuaded them to recognize him. He later found Paul in Tarsus and personally recruited him for the work in Antioch, where he could develop his teaching and leadership skills.

In the early years of their partnership, we see them addressed as "Barnabas and Paul," but as time went on they became known as "Paul and Barnabas" (see Acts 13:42). Paul was no longer the student but the leader, and Barnabas, once the trailblazer, became the nurturer.

Look up 1 Thessalonians 5:11 and write out what it says about encouragement.

Who has God put in your life as an encourager, or "God with skin on"?

Who is God laying on your heart to be a Barnabas (an encourager) to?

We enjoy and welcome encouragement from others, but at times God will take us out of our comfort zone to have us show encouragement to another. It may mean sacrificing something, but it is always worth the smile on the other person's face.

Look up Proverbs 3:27 and write out what action you're to take.

We are and will be surrounded by people who deserve our good, from our family members and friends to the unnamed person we meet at the grocery store. We also have the *power* to disperse that good to others when we see an opportunity to do so. It is our heavenly Father's instruction and expectation that we provide that good to those people at that time.

Delayed kindness is a lack of kindness. Delayed love is a lack of love. Delayed good is a lack of good. Delayed obedience is disobedience. If your son needs guidance with the challenges of life, don't put him off until you finish your household duties. If your daughter needs some attention because of the insecurities she's experiencing, don't put her off until you get all your shopping done. If your child needs some forgiveness, don't put that off until you get the apology you want. And if your child needs some discipline, don't put that off until you get all the rest you want.[13]

I know, I know. This won't always be easy and you may not have the energy to handle some things, but this is when you'll need to rely on strength and wisdom from God to keep moving forward.

To what or whom is God asking you to show good?

Look up John 15:11–14 and write out what love looks like.

What does it look like to lay down your life for someone?

You and I may not be asked to physically lay down our life for another. But as moms, at times we are asked to lay down our desires, dreams, and demands for a season. It's not always what we want to do, but this is called sacrifice, and God will honor our sacrifice.

> "Greater love has no one than this: to lay down one's life for one's friends."
>
> JOHN 15:13

While I was hospitalized when my girls were young, a dear friend, Sarah, helped John during the week. She brought all responsibilities outside her home to a screeching halt so she could watch our girls so they were able to stay in the security of our home. But it goes much deeper than this. Thirty years later, I can now look back and see all that one act of obedience produced through an ordinary woman who listened to a call from God.

Not only did her act of kindness impact our girls, but it was also an example to so many others of a woman listening to God's still small voice and obediently responding with a yes. She sacrificially took on the challenge with the power of the Holy Spirit's guidance for each day.

Little did she know the ripple effect her decision would have. She was not only caring for our girls, but also raising her two elementary-age boys and managing a home of her own. And it wasn't only for those months while I was hospitalized, but off and on over the next fifteen years through my multiple surgeries. Today, she is still a big part of our girls' lives—it's a bond that will not be broken.

What is God asking you to say yes to?

What is God asking you to say no to?

What might you need to lay aside to fulfill what God is asking of you?

What have you been asked to surrender as a mom? Which of these sacrifices have been the hardest to give up?

No is not a bad word, and it needs to be said at times. Knowing your limits and strengths will help you decipher your best yes. Your yes will look different in the various seasons of motherhood. What you once said yes to may take a back seat in a new season of motherhood, so take into consideration your family and do what's best so you can keep a sane mind and stable home.

LET'S HEAR FROM OTHERS

Our younger daughter, Sarah, reflects about the woman who sacrificed her life for our family ...

Big Sarah, it's hard to even put into words all that you mean to me. You've been my mom, friend, and mentor when I've needed one. You were even my grandma for Grandparents' Day when you were in your thirties—haha! You have been so special to me over the years. You've made every birthday party, graduation party, and just about every other family function. Encouraging prayers and letters from you over the years have been such a true testament of your love for God and others. I am so blessed to call you my "Big Sarah."

ACTION STEP

If *no* is something that God has been asking you to say no to, let today be that day.

If *yes* is something that God has been asking you to say yes to, let today be that day.

PRAYER

Dear Lord, help me to be sensitive to Your leading in my day-to-day activities and not become overwhelmed by my to-do list when You're asking me to do something for another. Help me leave margin in my life to make room for the yes (or no) You want me to say. I desire to be a vessel used by You in all I do. May my life glorify You whether it's through a private action or an action others see. In Your holy name, O God, I pray. Amen.

Day Five

BONUS MOM

Fervently love one another from your heart.

1 PETER 1:22

I couldn't think of a better way to end our week on connection than by reflecting on the importance of a bonus mom in your life and the lives of your kids.

Right about now, some of you may sound like a toddler, screaming, "Mine, mine! They're all mine!" You may not want to share your kids with others. And if you're honest, you get a little jealous of anyone who may want to steal your time with them. This is not a healthy attitude and is one that will need adjusting.

Or you may be the opposite and pawn your kids off on anyone who's available. This is not a healthy attitude either.

Today, we want to recognize the importance of others in your kid's lives—people who build deep, meaningful relationships that will contribute to the well-being of your children.

As I look back over the years of my girls growing up and the important "other" women in their lives, I'm so grateful that I wasn't the only one contributing to their development. Of course, as your children's mother, you have the largest role and influence on them, but grandparents also have a huge role in most cases. They're a natural extension of you. Next to you, grandparents are quite possibly the greatest influence your children will ever have.

Since most children's formative years are spent with mothers or mother figures, we're to transfer our faith and wisdom to our children. This isn't the job of the daycare, the school system, your friends, the television, or video games. Children ought to receive godly training at home and then, through some of the other systems, there can be an extension of your principles. This is also where a bonus mom comes in. You may have other "moms" in your children's lives and/or you may be a bonus mom for your bestie.

A bonus mom is another mom who has your back; she's there for you and your kids. She'll not only cheer you on but will also cheer on your kids. She'll show up when your days are hard, and may even swoop your kids away so you can take a much-needed nap. She loves your kids as if they're her own. She lays her life down for you and your children.

Your bonus mom may be your very own sister, a friend, or a woman twenty years your senior. Or you may be a bonus mom to your stepchildren. No matter where you and your friends find yourself, the role of a bonus mom will make a difference in the lives of your children.

Do you have a bonus mom in your life? If yes, share an important occasion your bonus mom showed up for.

Look up Titus 2:3–5 and write out what *other women* in our lives are to encourage us with.

Bonus moms were such a big part of my kids' lives. Even now that my daughters are grown, these moms still want to hang out with my girls and me when we're together. Our girls seek out lunch dates and visits with them, and they now mentor some of our friends' daughters. These women have become the Titus 2 woman to both our girls and now our grandkids.

Having friends and family who live out their Christian walk is the greatest influence on your children. Words are not even needed at times; it's their faith walked out that is an example of their inward beliefs. In addition, you'll want to be this woman to your kids' friends as well. You may be the only positive influence in their lives. You may be the only Jesus they meet. It may mean leaving the laundry for another hour, hanging in the kitchen with them as they eat the cookies you made, or taking a nap so you can stay up with them when they return from college.

If you're like me, you want your home to be the place your kids and their friends want to hang out. It may mean your schedule changes for a Friday night, but you'll have other Friday nights. It's important that you're visible for them to see—not all up in their business, of course, but available if they need you.

With this in mind, let's consider the relationship between Jonathan and David once again. This time, I want you to see the importance of the power of applause.

> Older women likewise are to be reverent in their behavior, not malicious gossips nor enslaved to much wine, teaching what is good, so that they may encourage the young women to love their husbands, to love their children, to be sensible, pure, workers at home, kind, being subject to their own husbands, so that the word of God will not be dishonored.
>
> TITUS 2:3–5

Look up 1 Samuel 23:13–18 and match the qualities of the good relationship between David and Jonathan.

1 Samuel 23:16	**Verbal encouragement**
1 Samuel 23:17	**Common faith**
1 Samuel 23:18	**No competition**

Here we see the power of applause through the relationship between David and Jonathan. One friend's encouragement gave strength to another to move forward. Jonathan strengthened

David through word and deed. British preacher Charles Spurgeon put it this way: "Any man can selfishly desire to have a Jonathan; but he is on the right track who desires to find out a David to whom he can be a Jonathan."[14]

There's so much we can take away from this friendship. A whole study could be written about the many aspects of their relationship. Jonathan nurtured a spiritual bond, showed sacrificial love, and offered encouragement and protection while harboring no jealousy. Having a Jonathan in your life is wonderful, and you're so blessed by that relationship.

Being a Jonathan is a whole other story. *Being* a Jonathan is a sacrificial intention you bring to a relationship, that starts with joining yourself to the Lord and becoming one spirit with Him (see 1 Corinthians 6:17). It's an attempt to see others as Christ sees them.

To whom may the Lord want you to be a Jonathan?

Write out 1 Thessalonians 5:11.

What are some ways you can build up another mom?

We never know all that someone is going through, and that is why, at times, we need to cut the other person some slack. All our friend may need is an encouraging, "Good job!" There are women who need to know we notice them. While observing their efforts, let's give them a shout-out. The power of applause will go a long way.

If you see your fellow sister loving her husband well—exalt her.
If you see her rearing her children in the admonition of the Lord—praise her.
If you see growth in your friend in an area you knew she was struggling—encourage her.

If you see a younger woman go after her dreams—support her.

If you notice a friend's cute outfit—compliment her.

Wishing others well will help you feel better about yourself and you'll brighten another's day (or maybe week).

I believe Christian women can have all types of friendships—both godly friendships and friendships with those who don't have a strong relationship with the Lord. However, I do believe our closest friends should be the ones we share a common faith with. Our standards of parenting will align better. We may not agree on everything and will need to make allowances for one another, but we'll be more on the same page with our beliefs and convictions. These are the women you want building into your kids' lives on a more daily basis, so choose your friends wisely.

Surround yourself with people who appreciate you for you! Make a practice of keeping company with those who want the best for you and will have your back. Stop wasting time trying to convince others to accept you. You need cheerleaders, not projects.[15]

You want your children's bonus mom to be a role model for your kids. You want her to be an extension of you. The people around you have a direct impact on what happens in you, so when you're choosing who to surround yourself with, it's essential that you choose people who are like-hearted.

Now, one last character trait of importance for you and your children's bonus mom.

Look up Proverbs 11:22 and write out the important quality trait this passage describes.

I know that picturing this may seem funny, but it's the truth. Beauty isn't much if the woman with it doesn't know how to act. It's hard to appreciate a gold nose ring on a one-thousand-pound potbelly pig! But this is a fair comparison to an attractive woman without personal grace being in pleasant company. Solomon knew the danger of this type of woman, so he warned his son against beautiful women, unless they also had the discretion and virtue that made them desirable companions.

Oh, Mama, desire to be put together not only on the outside, but also on the inside. And require that of your children's bonus mom as well.

LET'S HEAR FROM OTHERS

Christine shares ...

As I pondered what the words *bonus mom* meant to me, I realized that I could point to so many of these special women who have helped shape the person I am today. These women, all in their own different ways, were there for me during some of the best and worst times in my life.

When I was growing up, my mother had to work full-time. She was blessed to formulate some of her best friendships at her place of employment. These women became my family. They were there for me when I was having disagreements with my mother. They didn't judge or lecture; they listened and offered advice and a sympathetic ear. They told me when I was wrong, and they assisted in negotiating compromises between my mother and me better than the best lawyers could have.

They were fun. They took me shopping, to the movies, and to buy makeup, and taught me how to drive. They were there for break-ups, for new relationships, for teenage-girl drama, to celebrate my successes, and to help pick up the pieces when everything was falling apart. They were there for my wedding, to babysit my children, for funerals, and for everything in between.

As I transitioned into motherhood and developed my own lifelong friendships, I found myself blessed to not only have the best bonus moms for my daughters, but to also be fortunate enough to take on the role for their children. These girls, whom I love as my own daughters, have grown into wonderful, caring, godly young women. They text me just to see how I am, and to tell me they're praying for me and my girls. They send me fashion ideas and clothing items they think I need to buy for myself (these are common texts among us, as they know my love of shopping, much to my husband's dismay).

They let me know when I should be aware of things happening in my girls' lives that may need my attention. They reach out to me when they think I should know something about their mom so I can be there for her. They vent to me, they cry to me, and they share their best news with me. They reach out to me for advice in their careers and in raising their children.

We go shopping, go to spas, and have birthday parties. We're there for the best of times as well as the worst of times. We would each drop everything to be there for any emergency. They have taught me how to be a better mom to my own daughters by showing me different perspectives, and I thank God for allowing me to pay it forward for the great examples He put in my path when I needed it most. I'm so grateful that He's allowed me the fortune of playing this role, and that He's put the best bonus moms in my girls' lives.

 **ACTION STEP**

Seek out that friend God is calling you to be a Jonathan to this week and bless her with a small act of kindness.

PRAYER

Oh Lord God, thank You for the women You've brought into my life who reflect You in their love for me and my children. Help me to not take them for granted and to appreciate them. You know there are times when I keep others at a distance. Open my eyes to be watchful for those who want to befriend me, and help me be open to new friendships. In Your holy name, O God, I pray. Amen.

WRITE OUT YOUR THOUGHTS

WEEK THREE

You have made us
for Yourself, O God;
and our hearts are restless
until they rest in You.

ST. AUGUSTINE

Day One

A FATHER'S ROLE

Just as a father has compassion on his children,
So the Lord has compassion on those who fear Him.

PSALM 103:13

We've established that parenting takes more than just one person. No matter whether we're married or raising children as a single parent, it's important for others to help pour into their lives.

If you're a single mom, you may be tempted to skip this chapter, but please don't. Because no matter where you find yourself, it's important for your children to have a male role model in their life. A father, grandfather, uncle, or dear male friend can play a vital part in shaping your children into the people they'll become. The principles from this chapter should be implemented by their dad as well as other important male role models. Each is significant in its own way and will be a part of these people's roles in preparing your children to be responsible young adults.

Psychologists, both Christian and secular, will tell you the most formative years for a child is from birth to twelve years old. Our view of how we see the world and how we feel about ourselves is shaped by the family in which we grew up. As well, a father's or father figure's influence in a child's life is critical to their view of God as their Father. Children look for approval from their fathers. They want to be told they're enough. All kids do. And if they don't get that approval, they can spend a lifetime in emotional turmoil without even knowing it, seeking after it and never receiving it.[16]

Look up the following passages and match what it says about fathers and parenting.

1 Chronicles 29:18–19	**Pray for their children**
Proverbs 22:6	**Don't provoke their children**
Proverbs 13:24	**Discipline their children**
Luke 15:20–24	**Don't give up on their children**
Ephesians 6:4	**Be their child's first teacher**

It's the responsibility of both parents to train up their kids and be a living expression of Christ to them. However, children will look to their fathers to lay down the rules and enforce them. They also look to their fathers to provide a feeling of security, both physical and emotional. An involved father promotes inner growth and strength. But there are times, Mom, when you'll need to assist in making some of this happen.

Look up Genesis 2:18 and write out the establishment God made.

Ezer is the Hebrew word for helper used to describe this woman in Genesis 2. The common way in which the term *helper* is interpreted is to mean that Eve, unlike the other animals of the earth brought to Adam, was "appropriate for" or "worthy" of Adam and was to be his helper or companion on the earth.

Eve was not designed to be exactly like Adam (nor was Adam to be exactly like Eve). She was designed to be his mirror opposite, possessing the other half of the qualities, responsibilities, and attributes that he lacked. God made a woman a beautiful design in the image of Himself to be a strong support to her husband—not a competitor but a complementer.

> When was the last time you asked yourself, "How can I help my husband today? What will make my husband's day better?"

At times, you'll need to aid your husband with suggestions on how to bond with your daughter or son and encourage him to make time for them. Famous actor Ed O'Neill hit the nail on the head when he said that "90% of being a dad is just showing up."[17]

With this in mind, I want to share a reflection from a young woman, Mickey, about her dad:

> As simple as it sounds, the thing that stands out to me the most about my dad is that he has told me all my life, "I will always answer the phone when you call." No business meeting, luncheon, or activity was ever "un-interruptible." I am now in my early thirties and to this day, even if my dad is in the middle of something, he still answers my calls, makes sure everything is okay, and then lets me know when he can call me back. This seemingly small gesture has made me feel so important all of my life. But it isn't just the answering that has always made an impression; it's the way he answers and hangs up that lights me up. He typically answers the phone by saying, "How's my favorite daughter?" (I'm his only daughter), and more times than not, he concludes the call by saying, "I sure am proud of you!" He is my biggest cheerleader and, as you can imagine, the first one I call.
>
> One of my favorite memories of my dad was a month or so into my freshman year of college, when every single one of my new friends was asked to a fraternity event by upperclassmen. I was so devastated to not be invited and was so scared of spending the weekend alone. I'd been super homesick, and my dad sensed the sadness in my voice. He cleared his calendar and drove over six hours to spend the weekend with me. By the end of the weekend, I couldn't have cared less that I hadn't been asked to attend the event. Being with my dad was exactly what my homesick heart needed! Looking back, I think he might have been a little homesick for me too.

What I can tell you from watching my own husband is that he continuously tried to create memories and seize the moments he was given. And now he is doing the same with our grandchildren. I saw this in many ways ...

In the day-to-day activity—most days, he was home for dinner.

When we vacationed—he was ever-present and interactive.

As their coach—he tried his best to leave the role of coach at the field and become their dad at home.

As a disciplinarian—the girls knew when he was serious and they had a healthy fear of what he expected.

As a friend—well, that came later.

Encourage your husband to get in the photo and not just be a bystander.

Too many times in today's culture and on television sitcoms and movies, dads are depicted as incompetent, emotionally disconnected fathers and "secondary" parents who aren't nearly as important to their children as their mothers. This is what the culture pushes, but in reality, although a mother's love is important and special, having an active father figure plays an equally important role in the healthy development of a child.

Look up Deuteronomy 6:4–9 and answer the following questions.

Who does this portion of Scripture address (v. 5)?

What are you to teach (v. 5)?

Who are you to teach the principles to (v. 7)?

When and where do you teach the principles (vv. 7–9)?

If the Israelites were going to thrive in the Promised Land, the family unit would have to become the primary place where faith in and love for the Lord was modeled and transferred. Parents are to teach God's ways regularly in everyday events and in the ordinary days of life. While it's good for your family to have formal teaching times, it's equally important to welcome the Lord into all aspects of life. It will be how you transfer biblical worldviews so that God is their reference as your children navigate choices.[18]

What are some ways you've incorporated God into your everyday life with your children?

Going forward, how will you be watchful to incorporate God into your everyday life with your children?

This style of parenting will take time, effort, and a watchful eye. It's what we call intentional parenting. Work hard to instill the values and qualities you want your children to have that will successfully shape their lives.

If you're in a family where the dad doesn't play an influential biblical role, you as the spiritual leader in the family will need to step up to the plate and teach your children the biblical principles we discuss throughout this study. Your children need to hear the truths of God, and you are the perfect one to do it!

I like how The Living Bible describes women caring for their home in Titus 2:4–5: "These older women must train the younger women to live quietly, to love their husbands and their children, and to be sensible and clean minded, *spending their time in their own homes*, being kind and obedient to their husbands so that the Christian faith can't be spoken against by those who know them."

Mama, part of spending time in your home is making sure your children are hearing the Word of God and the principles of God.

LET'S HEAR FROM OTHERS

Alice shares ...

When I was raising my children, their father was not a big part of their daily or weekend lives. This was very difficult for them. I encouraged them to remember and lean into their heavenly Father, and that He would always be there for them. Having someone who is physically there for them was also important to me and needed by them. A role model, someone to teach them how they should be treated, was so needed, especially for my daughters. I was blessed to have three men step up and be there to teach them, pray with them, play with them, and love them unconditionally. Those men included the following: my father, while he was alive; Steve, a very close friend of the family and a devoted Christian; and their uncle Bill, my brother-in-law.

I encourage you, if you're in a situation where your children's father is not involved, or is sporadically in and out or just not able to be present in your children's lives for whatever reason, surround your children with role models they can lean into and look up to. The church, family, friends—it really does take a village to raise a child.

ACTION STEP

Be intentional about creating one-on-one time for your husband and your children, no matter their age.

PRAYER

Oh Lord God, I pray for my husband and his relationship with You. May he seek You with great fervency as he tends to our family. May his desire for his personal relationship with You grow deeper. Help me be a good help-mate to him and not be a stumbling block that will turn him away. Help us both to be all we need to be to each other and to be a beautiful reflection of You to our children. In Your holy name, O God, I pray. Amen.

WRITE OUT YOUR THOUGHTS

CONTROL THE CONTROLLABLE

For God gave us a spirit not of fear but of power and love and self-control.

2 TIMOTHY 1:7

We're living in an unprecedented time when we find ourselves holding our future and lives loosely in our hands. A quote from Corrie ten Boom has never rung so clearly than in the present days we're walking through: "Hold loosely to the things of this life, so that if God requires them of you, it will be easy to let them go."[19]

Our children are a gift on loan to us so we can train them up. At some point, we'll release them and become their sideline supporters.

I don't know about you, but I always say, "I'm a recovering control-freak." I'm not yet where I want to be, but I keep striving to let go of the desire to control everything. My family nailed it when they bought me a wooden plaque (which now rests on our fireplace mantel) that says, "As long as everything is exactly the way I want it, I am totally flexible."

Maybe you can relate.

Is God asking you to release the control-freak that lives in you?

Are you a mom who likes to be in control?

If we're honest with ourselves, we want to control most things. Now, organizing and planning are not bad characteristics to establish in life. However, if they block us from seeing beyond our own ideas and God's plan for our lives and the lives of our families, we need to reconsider the path in front of us.

I think one thing we've come to realize from living through the COVID-19 pandemic is that life requires flexibility. I believe, in theory, we know that flexibility is a strong characteristic of a committed mom and faithful friend. But, oh how the pandemic caused us to experience flexibility firsthand and take the concept to a new level.

Yes, there will be things in life that we're unable to control. But the one thing we always have control over is our attitude.

Look up Numbers 13:23–32 and compare the attitudes of the spies.

I want to have a Promised-Land attitude like Joshua and Caleb. Moses sent them into Canaan, along with the other ten spies, to survey the land for forty days. The ten spies had a wilderness attitude and were always complaining and seeing the negatives. But Joshua and Caleb had a positive attitude and observed the no-complaining rule. They had a *yes* attitude, the faith to see the bigger picture, and the ability to trust that God had all things under control.

Do you tend to have a wilderness attitude or a Promised-Land attitude?

What will you need to change to have a more positive attitude?

A positive attitude is contagious. I'm sure you've heard the saying "If mama ain't happy, ain't nobody happy." As moms, we set the temperature in the home and the family follows.

Years ago, I was preparing for a family vacation. John was finishing up work before our week away, and while I was frantically loading the SUV, I started to become resentful that I was doing all the packing. As I carried out the last few bags of everything we'd need for our time at the beach, I stopped myself and thought, *If I get in this car with the attitude I possess right now, it won't be good. We'll get off on the wrong foot, and my attitude will set the tone for the drive.*

> But flee from these things, you man of God, and pursue righteousness, godliness, faith, love, perseverance and gentleness.
> 1 TIMOTHY 6:11

So I took a deep breath and became grateful for the opportunity to go on vacation. With the help of the Holy Spirit, I was able to make the attitude shift from resentful to grateful. The power to do this lies with the Holy Spirit; on my own I'm incapable of possessing this attitude. But with the help of the Holy Spirit, "I can do all things through Christ that strengthens me" (Philippians 4:13) and so can you!

Instead of being resentful, I became grateful, and this change in attitude made the difference between a happy drive and a difficult one.

First Timothy 6:11 gives us a prescription for what we can control.

Look up 1 Timothy 6:11 and write out the things we should pursue.

So, what happens when we control the controllable—righteousness, faith, love, and endurance?

1. Foremost, it's a pursuit! A quest of following Jesus.

2. We seek His plans and not our own agenda. In addition, we realize the truths of Psalm 31:14–15: "But as for me, I trust in You, O Lord, I say, 'You are my God.' My times are in Your hand."

3. It unleashes us to become part of the process. We become moldable in His hands and move forward in what He sets before us.

4. We keep our eyes focused on Him and not our selfish desires.

5. Our perseverance and endurance comes from a strength beyond ourselves—the working of the Holy Spirit's power.

Controlling the controllable will take incredible commitment on your part. It's not for the faint of heart. So don't become weary in doing good. Control your pursuit of righteousness, stay committed to God's kingdom, and with intentionality seek to do His will. Strive to continue on in the strength of the Lord through the Holy Spirit's leading, and persevere!

Look up Psalm 37:5. What are you to commit to the Lord? And what promise is attached to your commitment?

I know, fully trusting God is easier said than done at times. But again, it comes down to controlling our attitude, mindset, and actions. We also mustn't allow the attitudes of others to control us. We want to be the difference in the lives of others. We want to be the person who helps others see the light at the end of the tunnel and the rainbow amid the storm.

By controlling the controllable, we actually show the watching world our commitment to Christ. A person can choose to be positive or negative, to be a creator or a complainer, to take responsibility or avoid it. Build on what you do have—strengths and assets—and don't complain about what you don't have.

- When everything within you wants to seek revenge, you can show love.
- When you want to curl up in a ball and not face the day ahead, you can display the joy that comes from your relationship with Christ.
- When the world is crumbling with discontent around you, you can be at peace because you know the God who holds the future.
- When that family member gets under your skin, you can demonstrate patience and show kindness even when it's not deserved.
- When your child speaks a harsh word, you can respond with a gentle answer.
- When others around you walk away from their convictions, you can stay faithful with yours and commit your ways to the Lord.

- When your flesh wants to do something not according to God's Word, you can have self-control because it's the Holy Spirit's control that overrides your fleshly desires.

Oh, wouldn't we live in a perfect world if everyone were controlled by the Spirit? Yes, it's our ambition to be controlled by the Spirit, but there are times when we fall short.

What do you do when you don't live up to the expectations of others or, for that matter, your own convictions?

When this happens, we start over! So let's control the controllable of seeking Him, walking worthy of our calling, and living out our days with a Christlike attitude.

Look up the following passages and write out how each one relates to control and the positive impact it has.

Proverbs 25:28

Matthew 6:34

Romans 8:28

2 Timothy 1:7

So, Mama, self-control isn't bad unless you allow it to become a god in your life and you're not able to exercise flexibility. Practicing self-control over your heart, mind, and actions will not allow the enemy a foothold. Let the Holy Spirit grow the fruit of self-control in your life.

LET'S HEAR FROM OTHERS

Sue, a woman who likes to have life under control, shares ...

I fall into the trap of "expecting" certain results from my efforts. However, even if I do everything "right," I still don't have the power to control the outcome. God gives free will. He is the perfect Father, but Adam and Eve still messed up. Living life with "anticipation" instead of "expectations" has been key for me to experience joy and peace in all things. All I can really control are my actions and reactions (my attitude).

One of the tools I use to help me practice self-control over my heart, mind, and actions is "TTR": T = Trigger, T = Thoughts, R = Reactions. As I began to take note of the triggers that led me to certain undesirable responses in my heart, mind, and actions, I started to identify the thoughts that would immediately come to mind. It soon became very clear to me that those thought patterns caused me to respond and react in certain predictable ways. The Lord helped me to prayerfully determine how I could change my thought patterns to bring about a more desirable reaction and response. I found that He also began to change the desires of my heart!

 **ACTION STEP**

If you find you're trying to control a particular situation or person, find the area that needs to be loosened up a little and do it. Remember, there will be some battles not worth fighting.

PRAYER

Oh Lord God, thank You for the abilities You've given me and for the way You have created me with the desire to do many things, but there are days when I leave You out. I want to yield control to You because what You do is better. Your ways are wiser. Your goals are grander. Your love is deeper. Thank You, Lord, for who You are and for not turning me away even when I'm bossy and controlling and domineering. In Your goodness, You simply remind me who You are, which reminds me who I am and helps me let go. In Your holy name, O God, I pray. Amen.

WRITE OUT YOUR THOUGHTS

Day Three

REST IS GOOD

Be still, and know that I am God.

PSALM 46:10 NIV

Is *rest* even in a mom's vocabulary?

I have heard this saying and probably you have too: "The years are short, but the days are long." But what does it actually mean?

It can be an encouragement to stay present through all the daily trials and the grind of raising kids or to not sweat the small things. However, whatever the reason, each hour seems to drag on. And some days you just long for your pillow and a few hours to yourself. But then when you get the opportunity to rest, guilt accompanies it. You think, *I should be doing* _____.

One particular summer day while I was out walking, the wild raspberries along the path were ready for picking and I couldn't pass them up. But while picking, I kept saying to myself, *I don't have time to pick these today.* Right before I stopped to pick, I'd been listening to a book on Audible. The author shared about rest, and I realized that some of my walks weren't really relaxing at all.

Let me just stop right now and say that this caught me totally off guard. What I thought was a breather in my day became, a lot of times, a continuation of my work. Now don't get me wrong, I continue to listen to podcasts and walk with friends. However, it was more of a mindset shift to enjoy the walk and some days to just walk in silence—or to stop and pick the raspberries without the guilt of being still.

Look up Genesis 2:2–3 and write out what was established and who established it.

Even God rested. So how much more should we make sure we give ourselves a margin to rest? Being still is hard for most of us in the twenty-first century, but discovering rest will energize you and fuel your tiresome soul for what lies ahead (and keeping up with your toddler).

What are some things you do to establish rest?

Do you ever feel guilty when you rest? If so, how do you handle that?

Rest can vary from an afternoon siesta, to a rocking chair on the porch with a glass of sweet tea in hand, to whatever stops your motion for a period of time. The hard part of exercising rest is implementing stillness and remaining consistent. Is "exercising rest" an oxymoron? When I wrote the phrase *exercising rest*, I thought I might need to edit it, but no. Because we definitely need to practice the art of resting.

As I observe my own daughters, now mothers, one of the many things I admire about them is that they've been able to implement rest into their daily schedules. It may not be every day, but while rearing infants and toddlers, they know the benefits of rest.

> You have made us for Yourself, O God; and our hearts are restless until they rest in You.
> ST. AUGUSTINE

In the early years of being a mom, sometimes you need to put yourself down for a nap, only because you don't get the needed rest through the night. At least not in the proper, normal sense when one would sleep in the dark for six to eight hours each night. No, your sleep cycle is most likely broken up into two or three installments. And then comes the teenage years, which is a different type of sleepless nights.

I remember saying to a friend as my daughters got older, "I can't keep up with my girls' schedule. I'm so tired at night!" She said to me, "Take a nap during the day so you can stay up with them at night."

There it is again—happy nappy!

Look up Hebrews 4:11 and write out what you need to be diligent in doing.

Yes, it will take a concentrated effort on your part and a willingness to stop and pick the raspberries, or smell the roses, or seize the day. Life is short. Don't miss the opportunity to enjoy the fruit of your labor and rest in the arms of Jesus daily.

St. Augustine wrote in his book *Confessions*, "You have made us for Yourself, O God; and our hearts are restless until they rest in You."[20] Aren't there days when you seem to wrestle with the idea of stopping and you never quite achieve what you have set out to do—like rest? Yup, me too.

Look up Psalm 46:10 and write out the command given.

I like the NASB version of this verse: "Cease striving and know that I am God." *Cease* means to sink, relax, or withdraw.[21] It reminds me of a person sinking down into a chair to relax. You can picture it, right? That comfy-cozy chair you love to recline in while wrapped in your favorite blanket—you settle down to rest, read, or binge-watch Hallmark movies. It's where you find relaxation and enjoy peace and calmness. In other words, it's a time to stop and ponder what God has done for you, while you lower the noise of the world.

You and I must be intentional in turning down the volume of the world if we want to be able to more clearly discern the voice of God and be able to hang with our kids.

Look up Matthew 11:28–29 and write out where you find rest.

If needed, what practical step will you take to incorporate rest into your schedule?

Jesus tells us, "Come to Me, all who are weary and heavy-laden, and I will give you rest. Take My yoke upon you and learn from Me, for I am gentle and humble in heart, and you will find rest for your souls" (Matthew11:28–29).

"Come to me and find rest." I know this can be a difficult concept to grasp and perform. God promises rest to those who will come, seek, and find it. Cease striving so hard and catch your breath from the daily grind while you refresh your soul in His presence. Breathe in God's presence as you sit quietly before Him and receive His gentle loving care to help you regain needed strength and rest for your soul.

He wants to meet you in the restlessness that can over-power you into a frantic frenzy of weariness at times. He longs to be the stillness deep within your spirit—the hushed strength that clamors for social acceptance. He wants to be the true rest that undergirds your stability in a chaotic world, providing the ever-present awareness that He is with you, beside you, and all around you, holding you and loving you with His outstretched arms.

> Jesus tells us, "Come to Me, all who are weary and heavy-laden, and I will give you rest. Take My yoke upon you and learn from Me, for I am gentle and humble in heart, and you will find rest for your souls."
>
> MATTHEW 11:28–29

When you have the opportunity, where (location) do you find rest?

Not only is rest vital for your personal well-being, but rest is important in the lives of your children.

Do you struggle to get your children down for their nap and/or is their nightly routine prolonged? If so, are there ways you can try to remedy this?

Do your pre-teens and teenagers get the sleep they need? If not, what can you do to help them get proper rest?

I know these routines can be interrupted and there are seasons that are more difficult than others. Sometimes, sleep is fought and becomes a battle. Other times, you wish they didn't sleep as much. Hang in there!

Sleep is just as important for children's growth, learning, development, and mood as it is for you. Sleep requirements vary from the infant to the teenage years, but establishing a good routine in the designated season will be beneficial in every season of childhood.

Here are some habits that may help your child sleep better at any stage:

- Keep regular sleep and wake times, even on the weekend.
- Turn off computers, tablets, and TV an hour before bedtime.
- Have a quiet and dimly lit place to sleep.
- Get plenty of natural light during the day, especially in the morning.
- Avoid caffeine in tea, coffee, sports drinks, and chocolate, especially in the late afternoon and evening.[22]

And here's one last passage.

Look up Psalm 121:1–8 and write out all the ways God is alert.

Thankfully, God doesn't slumber or sleep. He is our protection and guard, and is always watching over us. He will be the God who girds you with strength (see Psalm 18:32) when you feel weak. He will preserve your life, protect your mind, and guard your heart. We can rest in these truths!

LET'S HEAR FROM OTHERS

Nellisa shares ...

In my early years as a mother, I thought of rest as a failure to be productive. I was so wrong! As I matured, I realized that rest is vital. Rest is designed by God, for us. Rest is holy. When my children were younger, I would nap when they did, and rest brought me peace and re-energized me for the rest of the day. I also found rest in reading aloud while snuggling next to my littles. Now, in this season of my life, I spend much time in my car waiting for sports practice to end or a game to begin, and I try to always keep a magazine or book in my car. It's a great time to fit a little rest in. You can use it to pray, page through a magazine, read a book, walk, or whatever rest looks like to you. So go ahead and take your "holy nap." God wants us to rest.

 **ACTION STEP**

Be intentional about discovering rest this week. Set aside time to just be alone with God. Release yourself from the guilt of establishing stillness in your day.

PRAYER

Oh Lord God, thank You that You created rest and that I can be still and rest in Your goodness. Help me to trust in Your care for my life and take appropriate rest from work, trusting You to provide for me. Help me stop striving so hard, at times not allowing You to guide my days. And help me sleep and rest well each night, trusting You to watch over me and my children. In Your holy name, O God, I pray. Amen.

WRITE OUT YOUR THOUGHTS

Day Four

LASTING LEGACY

We will not conceal them from their children,
but tell to the generation to come the praises of the Lord,
and His strength and His wondrous works that He has done.

PSALM 78:4

When my grandmother, Jessie, turned ninety years old, I was asked to give a speech regarding her life. In front of fifty-plus people, I shared about her lasting legacy. It wasn't the money she would leave or the gifts she would distribute, but her love for family and her perseverance despite the deaths of two husbands, a daughter, and two adult grandchildren and sons-in-law.

It was her desire to live life to the fullest, which meant caring for those under her influence. She was always good at making people feel like they were the only one who mattered. Isn't that our desire—to make a mark on those who come after us, a spiritual watermark that never fades away?

I once heard pastor, author, and teacher Chip Ingram say on his podcast that parents should leave their children something money can't buy, as well as teach them how to suffer well, work unto the Lord, manage their finances, make wise decisions, and live grace-filled lives.

Now that's an inheritance.

We're not called just to leave something to those who come after us, but to leave something *in* them. Your children and grandchildren are only entrusted to you for a short period of time, and the legacy you will leave is the one you walk out every day.

What does legacy mean to you?

Read Hebrews 3:13–15 and write about the importance of today. (Don't put off until tomorrow what God is asking of you today! Tomorrow may never come.)

Write out Psalm 127:1.

The truth of Psalm 127:1—"Unless the Lord builds the house, they labor in vain who build it"—is foundational to us keeping our home intact and building a lasting legacy.

The most important part, when building a house, is the foundation. Our life is built on the foundation that determines its direction.

Read Matthew 7:24-27 and write out the contrast between the two foundations.

What are some ways you have built on the sand?

What are some ways you have built on the rock?

In this parable, Jesus tells us that when we build our house on a foundation of our own choosing, it ends up crumbling when the storms and trials come. When we build our own foundation, instead of a foundation that is Christ and His Word, we build it in vain. All the hard work we put in ends up collapsing from one thing or another.

As you lay on Jesus the foundation for your life and the well-being of your family, you allow Him to do the heavy lifting. When you let God construct the foundation, He is the one who ends up building your house and the direction of your life. When this happens, all things work for your good (see Romans 8:28), and when the storms of this life come through, you're still standing. You'll also begin to pray that not your will but His will be done (see Luke 22:42). You'll find your life is no longer built in vain, but on a foundation that will never fail.[23]

Look up the following passages and match them with the inheritance you desire to leave in your children.

Malachi 3:10   **Faith in the Lord Jesus**

Matthew 6:19–21   **Where true treasure lies**

2 Timothy 1:5   **Importance of tithing**

Colossians 3:23   **Doing the right thing**

James 4:17   **A good work ethic**

These are only a handful of Scripture passages that depict the inheritance we want to leave in our children. Again, you'll need to be intentional to instill these principles.

Look up Judges 2:8–10 and Psalm 78:4 and write about the contrasting difference found.

It's not that Joshua's generation intentionally dropped the ball. They didn't forget what the Lord had done for them (see Joshua 24:15–18). They just weren't purposeful about passing those stories on to their children, which resulted in a spiritual breakdown of the family and culture. This should be a sharp warning to us to take seriously the spiritual development of our children and share the goodness of God so it won't get lost.

How will you be purposeful in sharing the goodness of God with your children?

My friend and fellow author Eryn Lynum is the author of *936 Pennies: Discovering the Joy of Intentional Parenting.* She writes that on the day of their baby's dedication, she and her husband were given a jar of 936 pennies—a penny for every week until their child's graduation. They were instructed to remove one penny each Sunday as a reminder, and place it into another jar as an investment. Eryn goes on to say, "At some point every parent realizes time is moving swiftly, and they ask themselves, *How am I investing in my child?* Your goal as a parent is to discover how to capture time and use it to its fullest potential, replacing guilt and regrets with freedom. Meanwhile, your kids will see how simple choices, like putting the cell phone down and going on a family hike, will make all the difference. Together you can stretch time and make it richer."[24]

> A legacy is something that will follow you but must be built before we go.
>
> KIM COLLINGSWORTH

What practical ways will you intentionally build into your children?

Choose to live as though it was your last breath.

Love more deeply.
Forgive more promptly.
Give more generously.
Speak more graciously.
Care more thoughtfully.

In the end, it's what we do with Jesus that matters.

I want to remember this when my days speed by with little thought about my effect on others.

During my daughter Sarah's preschool days, I began to gain wisdom and have truth spoken into my life by Dora, a dear friend who would eventually go home to be with the Lord at 101 years old. I would pick up Sarah after her morning at preschool and head to Dora and Karl's house for our monthly lunch date, where she and I would sit and listen to stories of old.

When Sarah entered elementary school, I continued my visits with Dora; our time around the table was something I looked forward to. In her last years, Dora became more confined to her home and desired to have more purpose as she recalled her earlier days filled with activity and work for the Lord. I assured her that the younger women were still gleaning from her, learning to age with grace and poise and about the power of an effective prayer life.

It wasn't her accomplishments that impressed me or the recipes we exchanged, although those were good too. It was her love for her husband, her family, her grandchildren, and her great-grandchildren. It was her endurance through illness when I wasn't sure she would make it.

It was her trust in God to complete, with grace, what He had begun in her life.
It was the joy in her smile.
It was the twinkle in her eye when she reminisced about her courting years.
It was the kindness she would speak into her listeners' ears.
It was the preparations she would complete in their garden for the winter months ahead.

It was her desire to do good.

It was her respect for her parents as she matured.

It was her love for God's Word.

In the end, it's what we do with Jesus that matters. This is what I saw in Dora. Satisfaction. Contentment. Acceptance. Love. And her pursuit of righteousness, godliness, faith, love, perseverance, and gentleness (see 1 Timothy 6:11).

Herein lies the secret: Live a life of contentment. Stop desiring what you don't have and start being grateful for all you do have. An inner life of contentment will be evident to your children as they grow up. Instruct them to pursue righteousness over foolishness. This is a lasting legacy.

LET'S HEAR FROM OTHERS

Janel shares ...

I always tried to remember that the daily events around our house were directly linked to long-term development in our kids. While most of life is best described as ordinary, nothing is unimportant. Although we didn't always get this right, Troy and I knew that the legacy of relationships was being built by how we handled our disagreements. We knew we were building a legacy of work ethic, and so we insisted our kids finish what they started, even if it was just a few dishes. We were aware of the importance of raising honest adults and never wanted them to witness us "fudging" the truth. We knew the best way to instill humility was to openly acknowledge our shortcomings and be unafraid to ask their forgiveness, and we understood a legacy of faith would only be passed on if they saw it genuinely lived out in our lives every day. When we stay at it and are authentic, we build a beautiful legacy.

ACTION STEP

Consider the 936-penny challenge. Grab a mason jar and fill it with the number of pennies (a penny for every week until your child's graduation), then remove one penny each Sunday as a reminder and place it into another jar as an investment.

PRAYER

Oh Lord, help me love my children in view of eternity. Help me see the importance of pouring the love of Jesus into my children every day. May I desire to love more deeply. Forgive more promptly. Give more generously. Speak more graciously. And care more thoughtfully. In Your holy name, O God, I pray. Amen.

WRITE OUT YOUR THOUGHTS

Day Five

DE-PARENTING

But Jesus said, "Let the children alone, and do not hinder them from coming to Me;
for the kingdom of heaven belongs to such as these."

MATTHEW 19:14

I'm sure the last thing you have on your mind as a young mom is *de*-parenting. And for that matter, you may even be wondering what *de*-parenting is. I've looked high and low for a definition but haven't come across one. I guess I made up this word. (Not.) So here goes my best attempt at a definition for *de*-parenting—allowing your children to become independent while guiding them through decisions.

Basically, *de*-parenting is working yourself out of a job—you begin with the end in mind. Your child still lives under your roof, but you begin to step away from making their decisions and allow them to think through the process. You're not "all up in" their every move. Of course, you're still parenting and guiding them, just without micromanaging each action. As a parent, you must move from hovering to preparing your child to stand on their own two feet. Even more, you're preparing your child to stand before God, alone, to answer to Him on the basis of faith in Jesus Christ. God has no grandchildren.

Is *de*-parenting a new concept for you?

What is your definition of *de*-parenting?

It starts with baby steps. Your child moves from breast milk to bottle feedings. They move from sleeping in your room to sleeping in their own room. Soon, you don't have to pick out their clothes, as they're able to accomplish small tasks on their own. Eventually, your priority is to raise your child to the point that they're ready to be released from your full supervision.

In my life, it seemed like just when I started to get a grip on the whole parenting thing, I needed to begin to work on *de*-parenting. And yes, it is work. It's work to keep your mouth shut. It's work to allow them to choose what they're going to wear. It's work to let them take the car keys. It's work to step away instead of overhearing a conversation. Work, work, work—off to work you go. Motherhood has a learning curve.

What do you find to be the hardest aspect of *de*-parenting?

There's a shift that happens. Instead of "controlling" your child, you begin to see the need to "influence" them. You'll want to intentionally increase their freedom and their responsibility, and renegotiate restrictions, limits, and consequences with more flexibility. Of course, this comes with the trust factor based on your child's previous decisions. With more trust comes more *de*-parenting. *De*-parenting brings you one step closer to being your child's friend. But it's still not the season for full-blown friendship.

When I first discovered the concept of *de*-parenting, I thought to myself, *Wow. Is this a real thing?* I guess it was a wake-up call to the fact that my daughters were growing up. They were no longer the cute little girls with waterspout ponytails who I wished they could stay. They were in their teen years and beginning to look like young women. I was entering the other side of parenting, with more years behind me than in front of me. I couldn't stop it. You can't stop it either, as much as you wish you could. It's the natural progression of raising children to be responsible adults and to leave the nest.

What are some steps you can take to be an equipping parent?

What are some steps you can take to prepare your child to be a responsible young adult?

This was when I realized the importance of influence. I wish I could say that I thought more about the intentionality of influence a lot earlier, but I didn't. Don't get me wrong, I poured myself into my girls while raising them. I taught them right from wrong, good from bad, and lived intentionally in front of them—but the influence aspect hit me hard when I realized I only had five to seven years left with them living under our roof. And with intentional mentoring comes *de*-parenting.

Part of *de*-parenting is accepting this new stage of parenting and embracing it. After acceptance comes deliberate action, and *de*-parenting will become increasingly welcoming. You won't enter this new stage accidentally but intentionally. In the process, you'll need to equip yourself to slowly untie the apron strings that you tie while raising them, and prepare to *de*-parent gracefully.

What is your greatest aspiration for your child?

Look up the following passages and write down the important traits you hope to deposit into your children.

Ecclesiastes 2:26

Matthew 6:33

Mark 8:34–38

1 Peter 1:13–15

The traits you wrote down may not be what the world considers successful—for example, holiness, abundant life in Christ, seeking Him, and attaining wisdom, knowledge, and joy—but these are treasures in God's kingdom. The Bible gives us a much different picture of success that includes faith in Christ, obedience, stewardship, and Christlike character.

But sometimes the world's vision for success seeps into our parenting priorities without our recognizing it, and we begin to pursue priorities that take us away from the things the Bible prioritizes for the Christian life.

What are some worldly successes that can creep into a parent's mind?

What steps will you take to keep biblical priorities at the top of your list?

I'm sure some of the traits and ambitions you may have listed aren't bad in and of themselves, but they can easily become the main focus and take the place of the importance of living close to God.

I love the concept my friend Judy shares:

> As we were raising our kids, we focused on three key strategies: (1) We wanted to be equipping parents, (2) We wanted to be "yes" parents, and (3) We wanted to be encouraging parents.
>
> **As equipping parents**—our goal was to prepare them to be responsible adults capable of making wise God-honoring decisions, able to function in the world. Together, we worked through this process in learning certain skills:
>
> > *Step One— You watch, I do.*
> > *Step Two— We do together.*
> > *Step Three—You do, I watch.*
> > *Step Four—You do on your own.*
>
> We started this at a young age by doing laundry and cleaning the house. Each of the steps had to be mastered before the next was attempted. One time I skipped from step 1 to step 4 when I was in a hurry because company was coming. I asked the girls to wash the kitchen floor for me while I was busy upstairs. When I came down, both girls had their shoes off and were "sock skating" through the puddles they'd made on the floor. In their naiveté, they thought this was a more effective way to wash the floor. Needless to say, I learned my lesson.
>
> **As "yes" parents**—As the kids got older, we told them we wanted to be "yes" parents, saying yes to them as often as possible, but there were three conditions for us to say yes. First, they had to prove to be trustworthy. Second, we had to trust the situation. And third, the situation had to be doable.

These principles were applied in many instances, such as learning to drive a car. When they wanted to make the hour drive back to our former church for youth group, we allowed them to do this because we both trained and trusted them. We made sure the situation was not hazardous and was doable because we had a car available. As they got older and wanted to drive home after midnight, we had to tell them no. Although we trusted them, we didn't trust the situation with other drivers on the road at that hour.

As encouraging parents—We encouraged our kids to believe that they could be successful in life as they followed the Lord and the guiding principles they learned. Talking through both their successes and failures provided great opportunities to encourage them and further strengthen our relationship. Now that they're young adults, we've been pleased and blessed by their ability to function as mature young adults.

Which of these three strategies will you implement into your parenting?

As time goes by, you'll begin to see your kids blossom right in front of your eyes with their newfound freedom to make decisions. Their decisions will not always be the right ones, but providing them with guidance will give you the opportunity to help them deal with the fallout as well as the successes. You have to give them room for failure, heartache, and disappointments. This will provide the opportunity to help them process the difficulty in a mature manner and handle praise and success in a God-honoring way. Both success and failure build into the destiny of who they will become.

What is the hardest part of watching your child fail and experience heartache or disappointment?

Share a story of when you had to allow your child's failure or heartache to teach a valuable lesson.

De-parenting also makes room for you and your husband to have more time with each other, since you won't be accompanying your kids on every outing. I've heard from so many young moms that they get lost in their children and focus more on them than on their relationships with their spouses. Mothers sometimes prioritize their kids over their husbands, which can so easily happen, so you'll need to be super-cognizant about setting time aside for your spouse. Eighteen years go by in a blink of an eye and then it's just you and him again. Make sure you're still friends and you don't stop falling in love with each other.

Yale psychologist Elizabeth Rubin sees many couples who are reevaluating their relationships at this post-parenting transition. For couples who've kept their bond strong and their spark alive, grown children's departure can present a positive opportunity and a renewal of passion. But, she adds, some couples have difficulties because the kids have been their focus, and now they're looking at their own lives, including their marriage, and may not like what they see. About 25 percent of divorces in the United States occur after twenty or more years, often at this kids-to-college crossroads, and for those over fifty, that number has doubled since 1990, according to a 2012 AARP study.[25]

What are some ways you can prioritize your husband?

I know that some days this can feel like another task to fit into your day, but it will build up your marriage and be worth fighting for.

LET'S HEAR FROM OTHERS

Diane shares ...

I can honestly say I've enjoyed every stage with my four kids, even (and especially) now that they're all adults, but de-parenting wasn't easy. As our kids get older, the stakes get higher. It was especially difficult to watch my teenage daughter make decisions that weren't in her best interest. During that time, God was working through friends that strengthened me and prayed for me, and one friend in particular said three words I've repeated in my heart countless times since: "Just love her." So in my quiet moments, I prayed to God, I trusted God, and I gave her to God. And in my time with her, I bit my tongue and, although I didn't stop guiding her while she was at home, I focused on loving her above all. God definitely had His way in His timing—twenty-five years later, my daughter has made some tremendously good decisions and she and I are now truly friends.

Another challenge in de-parenting is resisting "peer-pressure parenting," even (or especially) within the church. Watching my kids make mistakes when other parents were stepping in and solving problems for their kids was especially hard, but I knew that my kids needed to learn how to navigate for themselves. Finally, although I felt deeply fulfilled in my calling as a full-time mom, I continued to maintain an identity separate from my kids—my identity in Christ, with my husband, with friends, and other interests—so that my kids would feel free to leave, grow, and become the unique individuals who God called them to be.

ACTION STEP

Take an everyday task and include your child: Step One—You watch, I do. Step Two—We do together. Step Three—You do, I watch. Step Four—You do on your own.

PRAYER

Dear Lord, help me to let go when all of me wants to hold on. Open my eyes to the new stages of parenting when it's time to allow my child to walk in a new way. I ask You, O God, to watch over this dear son or daughter. Heavenly Father, as a parent I know that I can't be with my children all the time but You can. Just like they feel the warmth of the sun shining on them, please allow them to experience Your presence. Thank You for being with them wherever they go. In Your holy name, O God, I pray. Amen.

WRITE OUT YOUR THOUGHTS

The "equipping parents" process of learning certain skills:

Step One—You watch, I do.

Step Two—We do together.

Step Three—You do, I watch.

Step Four—You do on your own.

JUDY COOPER

WEEK FOUR

Love

Others in

View of

Eternity

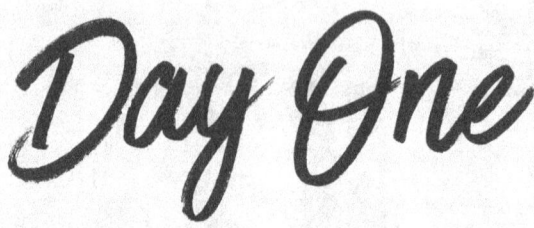

FAMILY TIES — A WIFE'S ROLE

Wives, be subject to your husbands, as is fitting in the Lord.

COLOSSIANS 3:18

This week we're going to look at the different roles within the family—for us as wives and for our husbands and children. Today we'll look up more Scripture than the other days, but I believe these passages are needed to support the topic of submission (haha). But before we move on to our relationships within our homes, let's explore how each of us are to do the work before us.

Look up Ecclesiastes 9:10 and Colossians 3:17 and write out how we are to do our work.

How do these verses speak to you?

Oh, Mama, we're exhorted to do *everything* as a representation of Jesus; in fact, Paul tells us to do it in His name, in His stead, and in His Spirit. Someone once put it this way: "We are the only Bible some people may read." This doesn't mean that we live our lives in fear that we may say or do something that misrepresents Christ. We're not supposed to be controlled by a spirit of fear but by a spirit of thankfulness (see 2 Timothy 1:7; Philippians 4:6). You may never write a book, but by living for God you will be one! We will be open books, "epistles of Christ," for all to read.

Read Ephesians 6:5–9. What do these verses reveal about how we can be like Christ on a daily basis?

Wow! We should long to represent our Father just as Christ represents God. When we realize that our actions should represent our heavenly Father, it will make us stop and think about what our motives should be.

One day, while preparing for a teaching from my book *Raising Girls: Diaper to Diamond*, I was sitting outside a quaint coffee shop in Boulder, Colorado. The table hugged the street that went through the shopping village. An SUV pulled up next to me carrying a mom along with three kids who were in car seats or booster seats in the back seat. What I heard while she was stopped at the stop sign—foul language loud enough for everyone around to hear—stunned me.

Now don't get me wrong, we all have bad days and wish we could take words back, but this was a good reminder to me that what's in our hearts will come out of our mouths (see Matthew 15:18). And the way we respond and act will be the way our kids respond and act. It's one thing to yell at our kids, but another to use unbecoming language. Be careful! The way we talk and act represents Christ.

As we look at relationships within the family, may we remember that as Christians we're representatives of Jesus Christ.

> "But the things that come out of a person's mouth come from the heart, and these defile them."
> MATTHEW 15:18 NIV

Although Paul may be brief in his discussion of the Christian principles in the book of Colossians, he certainly gets to the point.

Read Colossians 3:18–20. Identify the action verb Paul uses to show how each member of the family should behave. (I'll help you with the first one; it may be hard for some of you to write.)

Wife _____*Submit*_____ Husband_____ Children_____

Okay, Mama, before you want to throw something at me or skip over this section (or both!), let's see what submission really means. Although my thoughts will be primarily directed at married women, I believe this subject is pertinent to those who are single as well. The Bible also deals with the topic of submission in relationships besides marriage—to employers (1 Peter 2:18), pastors (Hebrews 13:17), and civil government (Romans 13:1–7). While submission may take a different form in these relationships, many of the principles still hold true.

How do you view submission?

In the Colossians 3 context, *submit* refers to a call to recognize and respond to the God-ordained authority of the husband or another authoritative person. Thus, God calls for submission between equals. Married women are not supposed to submit to all men, but rather to their own husbands. Conversely, married women should not seek leadership from other men apart from their husbands, no matter how worthy they are of honor or respect. They must rather be subject to their own husbands.[26]

Let's begin by looking at Christ Himself. He is the model for equality with God and submission to the One to whom He is equal. Jesus Christ, although equal with God the Father, submitted to Him to carry out the plan for salvation. Likewise, although she is equal to man under God (Genesis 1:27), the wife should submit to her husband for the sake of their marriage and family. Submission involves mutual commitment and cooperation and is a beautiful depiction of the Godhead.

Read the following verses and write out what each one depicts about Christ in relation to His Father.

1 Corinthians 11:3

1 Corinthians 15:28

Now read Ephesians 5:21–24 and describe the relationship between our husbands and Christ.

In her book *Feminine Appeal*, Carolyn Mahaney says, "God reveals His ultimate intention for submission in marriage: It is to reflect the relationship between Christ and His church. The husband is to mirror the sacrificial love of Christ by laying down his life for his wife, and the wife is to exemplify the church's joyful submission to Christ by following her husband's leadership."[27]

Read 1 Peter 3:1–6. What truth is shared in verse 1?

Of course, there are moral limits to this submission. According to Colossians 3:18, a wife's submission to her husband is only "in the Lord." That is, she is not obligated to follow her husband's leadership if it conflicts with scriptural commands or dishonors God in any way. We must never follow our husbands' leadership into sin. Our preeminent authority is God Himself.

So, dear sister, before we can submit to our husbands, we must first submit to God. Without submission to God, submission to one's husband does not constitute a spiritual exercise.

Share a "submission" story of your own.

Now, I'd like to expand on two questions asked in last week's work: "How can I help my husband today? What will make my husband's day better?" Is there something you've wanted to do for your husband but you just haven't gotten around to it? Well, today is the day! Go for it and see what your husband's response is.

Look up the following practical ways to love your husband and match them with the correct action.[28]

Proverbs 12:25	**Physically love him.**
Proverbs 21:5	**Plan for him daily.**
Proverbs 31:15	**Prepare for him daily.**
Romans 12:10	**Respect him.**
1 Corinthians 7:3–5	**Praise/encourage him.**
Ephesians 5:33	**Honor him.**
Titus 2:4	**Pray for him daily.**
James 5:16	**Show love to him.**

Wow. How many of these actions would you say you practice on a daily basis? A weekly basis? Or on any basis? I believe that if we begin to practice these truths, we'll begin to see a difference in our relationships with our husbands. Subsequently, this transformation would extend to our families and relationships outside our homes.

LET'S HEAR FROM OTHERS

I want to share a story about submission from my own life. We had lived in our first home for twelve years, and I loved my neighborhood. We raised our two daughters through elementary school, our neighbors nursed our family through my illness, and bonds of friendships were made. But due to some changes in the township, the residents voted to build a major grocery store chain just outside our backyard.

My husband, John, decided it was time to look for a new home. The house-hunting process happened very quickly, but with each day my desire to move was waning. I certainly agreed that I didn't want our backyard to change, but I also didn't want my neighbors to change. Within three months, we sold our home and began to build another one.

For several years prior to this move, I'd felt God calling me to begin a neighborhood Bible

study, which never came to fruition for one reason or another—or maybe just out of pure fear, I don't know. But I said to God, "If we make this move, I'll begin the neighborhood Bible study in our new neighborhood." So, after being obedient to my husband with the move, I now needed to be obedient to my God.

For the first six months we lived in our new house, I walked our neighborhood, prayed for families in the eighty-plus homes, and began to build relationships with the women. That fall, I sent out invitations to all the women and the neighborhood Bible study began with five of us. Through the years, it grew to over twenty women whose lives were changed by a relationship they formed with Jesus Christ. Praise the Lord!

Out of submission to my husband and to my God, I was blessed beyond what I could have ever dreamed or imagined.

ACTION STEP

Choose one action from the practical ways to love your husband and implement ways to show your love to him this week.

PRAYER

Oh Lord, bless our marriage with peace and happiness, and make our love stronger for Your glory and our joy both here and in eternity. Heavenly Father, I come before You to thank You for all You've done and continue to do in our lives and marriage. Help me be the wife I need to be, and help me to see the good in what my husband does. Help me to be patient when everything in me wants to control a matter, and give me loving words when I need to confront a situation. In Your holy name, O God, I pray. Amen.

WRITE OUT YOUR THOUGHTS

Day Two

FAMILY TIES — FATHERS' AND CHILDREN'S ROLES

Husbands, love your wives and do not be embittered against them.
Children, be obedient to your parents in all things, for this is well-pleasing to the Lord.
Fathers, do not exasperate your children, so that they will not lose heart.

COLOSSIANS 3:19–21

Although our husbands are not participating in this study, it's good for us to look at what the Bible says about the roles of fathers and children.

Read the following passages. For each, write out how husbands should relate to their wives.

Colossians 3:19

Ephesians 5:21–33

1 Peter 3:7

Husbands are supposed to exercise loving leadership, not dictatorial dominion. Both men and women need the reminders that we've looked at over the past two days. Men need to remember to be tender and loving as much as women need to remember not to usurp the rightful, God-given authority of their husbands. So, in a maturing marriage the husband exercises compassionate care and the wife responds by willingly submitting to his loving leadership.

What does 1 Peter 3:7 say will be hindered if the husband does not treat his wife lovingly?

A living relationship with God depends on right relationships with others. If men use their position to mistreat their wives, their prayers will not be heard. This principle not only holds true for family relationships, but also carries over to all relationships.

Read Matthew 5:23–24. What are you supposed to do if you have a grievance with someone?

I know some of you working through this study may have a husband who isn't living as the Bible instructs. And then there are others of you who are blessed to have a God-fearing man at your side. Wherever we find ourselves, our desire should be to continually pray for our husband. Talk with him, not at him. A lot of times it's the way we approach him that sets the tone for the conversation. Remember that you and he are both a work in progress and God will forever be working on you.

Look back at Ephesians 5:21. Who does it say should submit?

At times, our own insecurities hinder us in our connection with our husband. You'll both need to yield to Christ before yielding to one another to show value and respect. However, if your husband is leading you into sin or away from the Lord, please be sure to talk with someone like a pastor or Christian counselor and get help navigating through your particular situation.

Boy, do I royally mess this up at times and not approach a conversation or a situation in the way I should. I think we all do at times. I really love the advice that friend, author, licensed chaplain, and board-certified pastoral counselor Bethann Miller gives in her book *The Invitation: Keys to Strengthening Your Marriage*: "Instead of arguing your point on something your spouse has articulated, pause and ask them to help you understand what they are feeling. This helps create a platform of emotional and relational safety."[29]

What would happen if you and your husband practiced yielding to one another?

What makes it hard to yield to one another?

How can you better understand your husband?

Now, on to the role of the children ...

Obviously, Paul's principles for children in Colossians 3 are for those who've reached the age of understanding. He tells them that they also must come under the rule of Christ.

Read the following passages. Identify the principles for children mentioned in each one.

Exodus 20:12

Proverbs 6:20–23

Ephesians 6:1–3

Disobedience to parents in the Old Testament was called rebellion against God and was severely punished (see Exodus 21:17; Leviticus 20:9). In the New Testament, Jesus set an example for all children by obeying His parents, Joseph and Mary, when He returned to Nazareth with them after they found Him speaking with the religious leaders in the temple (Luke 2:51).

Obedience reflects God's design for order in the family. The fifth commandment in Exodus 20:12 is the first of the Ten Commandments with a promise: "that it may be well with you and you may live a long life on the earth."

> Fathers, do not provoke your children to anger, but bring them up in the discipline and instruction of the Lord.
>
> EPHESIANS 6:4

Years ago, I was listening to a sermon on children obeying and respecting their parents and I remember thinking, *Wow. I wish my girls were here to listen to this one.* By the end of the service, however, I realized that the sermon wasn't only for children being reared, but also for me as a grown child. Adult children also have a responsibility to the Lord: to respect their parents as they age. Obedience may take on another form as we mature, but respect never loses its grip.

It's a blessing when our children obey us and heed our advice, isn't it? Additionally, as parents, we play an important role in the family dynamics.

Look up the following passages and describe who they address.

Colossians 3:21

Proverbs 1:8

Proverbs 6:20

Only fathers are mentioned in Colossians 3:21 because they're the head of the house, but we can clearly see that the same principle applies to mothers as well, according to the verses from Proverbs.

How does Ephesians 6:4, along with Colossians 3:21, say fathers should care for their children?

As parents, we're not supposed to frustrate our children, because it will just stir up evil emotions within them. This will in turn discourage their love for the Lord. Praise for well-doing rather than constant criticism, along with loving discipline, will help you rear your children in the training and instruction of the Lord (see Ephesians 6:4).

Now, if you're like me, you've royally messed this one up at times too. So, what do you do about it? Begin again! Ask God to give you strength and wisdom, and watch for ways to praise and encourage your children.

In what ways do your family relationships need to change to make them pleasing to the Lord?

LET'S HEAR FROM OTHERS

Ginny shares ...

I am so blessed with a husband who shows me with persistence and consistency that he loves me. One of the things we have learned throughout our fifty-eight years of marriage is that it's the little things we do for one another that really matter. Just bringing me a cup of coffee or helping me make the bed says "I love you" in a really big way. The one thing that magnifies all this is that our children are watching. Many things are taught simply from the practical side of living life together. Did we always do it right? Not at all. But we always remember God is faithful. His promises are true, and what He brings to our home when we do it His way are love, joy,

peace, gentleness, and so much more. That's His promise. As Father Theodore Hesburgh says, "The greatest thing a father can do for his children is to love their mother."[30]

 **ACTION STEP**

Choose another action from the practical ways to love your husband from yesterday's homework—physically love him, plan for him daily, prepare for him daily, respect him, praise/encourage him, honor him, pray for him daily, or show love to him—and implement it.

PRAYER

Oh Lord, I pray for my husband's relationship with our children. May they be relationships that glorify You. Give him patience and strength to handle each child in a loving and respectful way. I ask for wisdom and humility in the face of the task of parenting. Give both my husband and me the strength to do well by our children and by You. In Your holy name, O God, I pray.

WRITE OUT YOUR THOUGHTS

Agape—Unconditional love

Philia—Brotherly love

Eros—Romantic love

Storge—Family love

Day Three

HE LOVES ME, HE LOVES ME NOT

But now faith, hope, love, abide these three; but the greatest of these is love.

1 CORINTHIANS 13:13

Do you remember that childhood petal game that was played with a daisy? We would grab a flower and begin plucking the petals, alternating the phrases "he loves me" and "he loves me not." The last petal picked would predict how that special person, in our mind, felt about us.

Now that we've grown up, it probably isn't a game we play anymore, but the concept is something most of us women still grapple with. It's an emotional back-and-forth of wondering if that friend still values us, if our significant other intentionally hurt us, or if our child really meant what they said.

This flip-flopping emotional occurrence may no longer hold the answer to our romantic destiny, but it does have a tight hold on our heart. It tends to influence us daily because, as hard as we may try not to, we care what others think and how they feel about us. So we find ourselves constantly interpreting gestures, words, and expressions of others, trying to figure out their intent.

When I find myself lost down this path of pleasing others, or I realize my thoughts are consumed with reading other people and interpreting their perspective of me, I know it's my responsibility to refocus my mind and meditate on truth. That truth is Christ. That truth is His great love for me. That truth is knowing the Father's love should be my measuring stick, not the love of others. Because when we rest in His unconditional love, we live in the freedom of His grace. With our eyes fixed on Him, others' opinions and emotions don't have the hold on our hearts they once did.

This type of love is what I desire for each child of God. It's the type of love you will want for your children.

Read Colossians 3:12–15 for your strategy to live for Christ day by day.

What should you willfully clothe yourself with?

According to verse 14, what is the most important thing to put on? Why?

It's been said that love is a color that can be worn with anything—overalls or an evening dress. Or you can think of it as a kind of overcoat, a garment that covers all other virtues. It brings harmony to all disharmonies. Love is the garment the world sees. All other virtues are undergarments.[31]

How well are you loving those in your family?

Is there an article of your clothing (a virtue) that is torn? List the steps you will take this week to begin to mend it.

Did you know there are different meanings for our English word love? We're going to explore what the Bible says about love—and there's a lot! I'd like us to explore the four Greek words for love and see how we can apply their meaning to our lives and relationships. The English language only has one word for love, whereas there are four types of love in the Bible: *agape*, *philia*, *eros*, and *storge*.

Look up 1 Corinthians 13:4–7 and write out what love is.

This passage from 1 Corinthians is one of the most popular in the Bible and may have been read on your wedding day. However, the Bible teaches us a different way to love. Love is about doing what's best for the other person, not always what's easiest. The Bible challenges us to not only love our friends but also our enemies. Our love must extend to those who don't deserve it. And if we're honest, there are days we don't much feel like loving the people under our roof or feel they warrant our love. Oh yes, there will be days when it will be easier to love than others. Many times I've thought, *I do love so-and-so, but today I don't much like them.*

Are there days when it's harder to love than others?

Following are four Greek words found in the New Testament that illustrate different aspects of love. We'll look at the meaning of each and see how we can apply them to our family relationships.[32]

AGAPE — Perfect and Unconditional Love

Agape is probably the most well-known of the four types of love, and it is the highest form of love. This divine kind of love can only come from God. Agape shows God's immeasurable and incomprehensible love for us.

Look up John 3:16 and write out how agape love is shown.

John 3:16 shows us how Jesus perfectly encapsulates agape love. God loves us because He is Love. And it's this perfect love that saves us. With the help of the Holy Spirit, we can experience and show this same kind of love. Agape love can be defined as the unselfish, self-sacrificing love that God has for His people.

We, as human beings in our natural fallen state, can't produce this kind of love because of the selfish nature we are born with as a result of the fall of mankind. The lack of this agape love, brought on by our own selfish desires, is the reason why most relationships, friendships, and marriages are not lasting.

If we want to love others selflessly, we need God's agape love in our life, which will enable us to sacrificially love others without any selfish motives. This is the love that gives of itself freely, without expecting anything in return.

What practical ways can you show agape love to your husband and family?

PHILIA — Brotherly Love; Friendship

Perhaps you recognize this word as the root of Philadelphia, also called the City of Brotherly Love. This Greek word describes the powerful bond between friends, so philia is the kind of love found in friendships.

Look up John 13:35 and write out how philia love is shown and what others will observe about you in the way you love.

Philia is the most general type of love found in the Bible, and is used to show how Christians should interact with each other. It's philia love that Jesus said should be the marker of His followers' lives. We should be known for this type of love that centers around care, respect, compassion, and deep connections with each other.

What practical ways can you show philia love to your husband and family?

EROS — Sensual or Romantic Love

Eros is the name of the mythological Greek god of love and sexual desire. Eros is also where we get our English word *erotic*. The Bible takes this Greek word and applies it to the relationship between a husband and wife. Promiscuity was rampant in Bible times, just as it is today, and the Bible continually reserves the eros love for marriage.

Look up Song of Solomon 1:2 and write out how eros love is displayed.

Song of Solomon proclaims a wholeness that is at the center of God's teaching on committed love for a world that seems to focus on lustful sex outside the confines of marriage. The Bible illustrates that men and women are created physically, spiritually, and emotionally to live in love. The love between a husband and a wife should be, among other things, an erotic love. However, a marriage based solely on erotic love will fail. The thrill of sexual love tempers and wanes. Healthy marriages will have what God intended: a mix of eros, agape, and philia—sexual, unconditional, and friendly love.

In what practical ways can you show eros love to your husband?

For many women, especially young mothers, this kind of love can end up feeling like just another to-do on your list. But it should be an aspect of your relationship that you take seriously and make a priority.

STORGE — Love for Family

This type of love is one that most are unfamiliar with. The Greek word describes the naturally occurring love family members have for one another. A parent can't help but love their child, and a child's bond to their parents happens without effort. Storge is a special, unique kind of family love.

Look up 1 John 3:16 and write out how storge love is displayed.

Although this verse doesn't use the word *storge*, it depicts familial love. Many times when Paul writes, he does so to his "brothers" and his "beloved" in one church or another. There's so much tenderness between fellow believers because they're united by the same Father in heaven. Followers of Jesus are part of God's family; we're knit together not by blood but by Spirit. Therefore we should love each other with the deep affection of storge love.

What practical ways can you show storge love to your husband and family?

Here are some practical ways you can show familial love to one another: pray and forgive one another, be a good role model, speak truth in love, and stick together.

LET'S HEAR FROM OTHERS

Vicki shares ...

To love as God loves can be a challenging assignment. How are we to not just love others but love them well? I struggled with this idea until God showed me that I start by loving Him first. As I grew in my knowledge of God's character, my love for Him grew, as well as my desire to live a life that's pleasing to Him. He tells us in His Word how to love our husbands, parents, children, friends, and enemies. In my prayers I began to ask God to help me love others as He loves them. Then I became more specific by naming whom I needed help loving. I continue to include these people in my prayers each day. By including love in my prayers, I can see God transforming my heart to be more like His.

ACTION STEP

Choose a practical way to show love to your children. It doesn't have to cost you much, just your time.

PRAYER

Oh Lord, I praise You that You're a loving and faithful God and that You first loved me. Help me to love You with all my heart and soul, and to love my husband and children the way You created me to love. I'm sorry for the times that I've fallen short of loving them the way You designed me to love. May Your love fill my heart so that I love out of the overflow of Your love for me. In Your holy name, O God, I pray. Amen.

WRITE OUT YOUR THOUGHTS

Day Four

THE DIFFERENCES IN YOUR KIDS AND HOW TO ADJUST YOUR PARENTING

Children, be obedient to your parents in all things, for this is well-pleasing to the Lord.

COLOSSIANS 3:20

When raising our children, we must come to the realization early on that they're not going to be mini-mes. Oh, they may have similar traits and personalities, but they're their own people. You may have one who looks more like you or one who favors your husband. You may have one who likes the same things you do or one who's preferences are very different. And for that matter, you may have children who are polar opposites. What do you do with that?

I believe we start out parenting from the same box. But fairly early on we begin to see the differences between siblings. Then we need to adjust our parenting style to each child's personality. What works for one may not work for another. Yes, we will treat them differently. We will parent them differently.

"Kids are all very different when it comes to emotional support," explains licensed clinical psychologist Kate Roberts, Ph.D.[33] There are vast differences in emotional intelligence. Some kids are gifted and catch onto things very early on while others develop typically or need more time. Some thrive with social interactions while others struggle.

A crucial component of parenting is figuring out your child's style and supporting them to develop a strong emotional skill set. It's not wrong to recognize these differences. In fact, it's required to be an effective parent.[34]

Write the name(s) of your child(ren) and each of their personalities.

Do you parent each child differently according to their personality?

One of your girls may like to play with dolls whereas the other likes to climb trees. One is sweet and the other is sassy. One of your sons may like to play with any kind of sports ball, whereas the other would rather read a book. One is an introvert, happy to do their own thing, and the other is an extravert who thrives on parties and team sports. Adventurous kids may cause your hair to gray early, but more timid children can worry parents as well, as they often need an extra push in life to make the most of their other attributes.

Biblical parenting involves encouraging, exhorting, and empathizing with children according to their unique needs and character. It's important to understand the personality God has given each of your children and how to tailor your parenting styles to meet those needs.

Look up 1 Thessalonians 5:11 and write out the ways a parent builds up their children.

Although my girls had kindred interests, their personalities were different. One hated to take the bus to school. The other sat right behind the bus driver to converse with him on the ride home. One kept a diary, the other didn't. One thrived on words of affirmation, the other on quality time.

Biblical parenting will take having a watchful eye on your children as they're maturing from baby to toddler, from toddler to elementary age, from child to teen, and beyond. Each stage will look different. Although, looking back now, I recognize my daughters' personalities were formed early on and didn't vary much from season to season. Yes, they matured and embraced their personalities and adjusted when needed, but for the most part they were the same little girls—all grown up.

Do you believe your children can be fueled by the way you love them?

What are some ways you try to fill your children's love tanks?

If you're not familiar with Gary Chapman's book *The 5 Love Languages of Children*, let me introduce you to it and encourage you to pick up a copy for your library. Through Gary's book, you'll be exposed to children's primary love languages: physical touch, words of affirmation, quality time, gifts, and acts of service. Every person will have a primary love language that goes straight to the heart, but it doesn't mean that the other four types of love should be completely eliminated or ignored.

As your child grows and develops, so will their love languages. There are no incompatible love languages, only opportunities to love each other.[35]

From this brief description of *The Five Love Languages*, write your child(ren)'s name and what you think their love language(s) might be: physical touch, words of affirmation, quality time, gifts, or acts of service.

In addition to knowing your child's love language and pouring into them, discipline will be an important part of shaping them. Their discipline will be determined by their age. "Young children need very little discussion when disciplined," explains licensed clinical psychologist Kate Roberts. "Just action—take away the video game, put them in another room, down for a nap, etc.—works. Older kids should be learning how to problem-solve and manage behavior better. Discuss strategies and approaches to internalize coping methods for behaving."[36]

There'll be times when you won't be patient with your children when they display inherent personality traits, especially if they're directly opposite your own. If you're quiet by nature, a nonstop chatterbox may annoy you, no matter how much you love her. Conversely, if you're sociable, you may lose patience with a shy, quiet thinker who has trouble expressing feelings and thoughts.

Likewise, a child with an inborn sense of fairness coupled with a strong will may want to debate every issue. That may drive you nuts—especially when half the time they're right. Consider how you and your child differ in terms of persistence and attention span, activity level, sensory threshold, mood and intensity of responses, approach or withdrawal, adaptability, and regularity. It's easy to see how problems can arise if you and your child differ in these areas, and just being aware of how your personality traits are different—as well as alike—can help you maintain your cool.[37]

> Train up a child in the way he should go, even when he is old he will not depart from it.
>
> PROVERBS 22:6

Write out Proverbs 22:6 and share what you believe this verse means.

Do you believe Proverbs 22:6 is a promise?

I remember reading this verse as a young mom and thinking, *If I do A, B and C, my child will turn out well.* Not so. There may be times when you'll do all that you think is best and your child still follows his or her own way. Then both parties need to learn grace. You may even be a woman who was a prodigal and have returned to the Father. If so, I rejoice with you and praise God that you are enjoying a renewed fellowship with God. 'Tis so sweet!

Some scholars try to scoot around the problem by contending that Solomon's proverbs are not promises, but there's another way to understand Proverbs 22:6 without undermining its promissory nature, and I've found that approach extremely helpful. Instead of it being a promise that "if you do right, then your kids will turn out right," it's a reverse promise. It's a warning that if you don't correct your children when they're young, then they will run amok, wanting their own way as adults. The clear warning of Proverbs 28:26—despite Disney's messaging—is that following our own heart, or our own "way," is the epitome of foolishness.

That's why Proverbs says that the parents' role is to correct their children's natural foolishness, and so Proverbs 22:6 is a warning that parents must discipline their children's foolish character before it is set.[38]

Look up Proverbs 4:12 and 28:26 and compare what these verses say about the foolish and prudent.

Certainly we as parents are always training our kids, even through our passivity. For example, by failing to lead them to repentance before our sovereign God, we teach them that they're fine to continue living as self-made kings and queens rather than servants. By failing to instruct them in God's commandments, we teach them that God's Word is *not* the highest authority in our lives. By failing to set boundaries, we instruct them that we really don't care whether they do good or ill.

So, Mom, yes, it is your job to help train your child in the way they should go. But consequently, Proverbs 22:6 implies that the parents' intentional moral and religious shaping early on will have a permanent effect on their child for good. This statement is not a hard-and-fast promise to parents, but the rest of Proverbs makes clear that the power of a child's future depends not only on the parents' guidance, but also very much on the choices he or she makes.[39]

Look up Proverbs 22:1–20 and write out the contrasts you see between righteousness and unrighteousness. (I'll help you get started.)

Verse 1 – Desire a good name over wealth.
Verse 3 – The wise notice danger and are careful.

In my Bible, next to Psalm 92:12–15 I have the words *2016 goal* written. And I pray the words of this Psalm will be your goal too.

Look up Psalm 92:12–15 and write out your personal goals as a woman of God, wife, and mother.

We can learn volumes from the beautiful illustration of the palm tree and the cedar in Lebanon. Like depicted in Psalm 92, both bear much fruit. Specifically, palm trees grow deep roots into the ground until they strike living springs. May we grow deep roots in Christ, drawing nourishment for our daily living and strength as we parent.

Along the same lines, cedar trees are strong and mighty. May we bear the unbending strength of a cedar as we call upon the name of the Lord for our power. Our flourishing and growth will continue into old age as we seek God for nourishment and might.

God has kept you alive and given you opportunity for fruitful living. Yes, fruitful living! So what are you going to do with it? Are you going to live your life to your fullest potential? Or are you going to settle for ease and comfort? What you do with the opportunities given to you is your gift back to God through your response, action, and commitment. You must continue to move forward. For, "whatever your hand finds to do, do it with all your might" (Ecclesiastes 9:10) and flourish right where you are planted.

Great job today, Mama!

LET'S HEAR FROM OTHERS

Melanie shares ...

Looking back after raising three very different children, I see that God gave me the wisdom to learn to parent each one differently while loving all of them equally. We taught our kids that life has consequences—that there are good consequences for wise choices and bad consequences for unwise choices. So, in parenting three very different kids, the consequence for misbehavior by my oldest child was losing a play date with friends, while my middle child would lose time on electronics and my youngest child would lose out on snacks for a period of time. The punishment for each one had to be losing something that was important to them at the time. My oldest child is a pleaser, my middle has always strived to be independent, and my youngest is a mix of both, so they received and responded differently to almost every situation. This challenge to success-fully parent each uniquely kept me on my knees in prayer!

ACTION STEP

Read *The 5 Love Languages of Children* by Gary Chapman and determine each of your children's love language.

PRARER

Oh Lord, help me to accept each of my children for their own personality and giftedness. Increase my love for each one, and give me a keen eye to watch for their differences. Provide me with the strength to fill up their love tanks with their specific needs. Help me to encourage them so that they will grow in strength and dignity. In Your holy name, O God, I pray. Amen.

WRITE OUT YOUR THOUGHTS

Day Five

THE FRIEND ZONE

Just as lotions and fragrance give sensual delight,
a sweet friendship refreshes the soul.

PROVERBS 27:9 MSG

Through my twenty-plus years of battling Cushing's syndrome, there were times when all I wanted was to be able to live long enough to raise my girls. And then came the next step: I wondered if I would ever get to the stage where we are now—friends.

Friendship with my daughters came while they were in college—definitely the climax of *de*-parenting. Theirs was such a sweet transition from girls to women, although it didn't come without the shedding of tears. When our older daughter, Lauren, left for college, there was a huge void in our home, especially around the dinner table. It was certainly a season I needed to wrestle through.

For the first couple of weeks after she left for college, I would go into her bedroom in the morning after waking up and lie on her bed, hug her left-behind stuffed animals, and cry. I missed her so much. I would lie there and think on the years we had with her and pray for the years she had in front of her. Some were tears of sadness while others were tears of joy. Eventually I came to embrace this stage, and watched her become independent, wise, and my friend.

Two years later, Sarah went off to college. I experienced the same loss as our baby girl left. Now I had two bedrooms unoccupied. Two rooms to lie in a bed and pray for them. There was just something about lying in their bed that somehow diminished the miles between us.

Sometimes, it is easy to forget that our children are only small for a very short percentage of their lives. If they're blessed to live to the age of eighty, they would have spent only 20 percent of their lives under the age of eighteen. The rest of the time, you'll both be adults (crazy, I know).

Be honest. Do you want to be friends with your children?

Do you think developing friendships with your children happens sooner or later in the seasons of parenting?

Strive to spend time with your children in ways they enjoy. Have them work with you and do chores, but also play games with them. Find music you both like and listen to it together. Find an excuse to take them on long car rides. Share inside jokes. Do things (age-appropriate) that you'd enjoy doing with your friends. Don't be afraid of being the kind of parent who your kid chooses to spend time with. And don't be afraid to raise a kid who you think is pretty fun to hang out with. Create fun within your home. I do believe when you do this, your kids will want to return to your home when they're grown. Our family motto is "A family that plays together, stays together."

God willing, your reward will be a lifetime of friendship with your children—a glimpse of the joy of heaven on earth.

What are some fun things you do with your family to build a strong bond?

I didn't have sons, but I do have grandsons. And yes, as their mimi, I want to be their very best friend. This stage does come a little sooner for grandparents, but friendship is still not for during the rearing stage.

Shortly after our first grandson was born, I was away speaking at a retreat and the woman organizing the retreat shared a story about her mother. As the speakers had been gathered together for prayer before the event started, the organizer received word that her mother passed away. It wasn't unexpected but was still devastating. Something she shared with us before she headed out for the long trip south stuck with me.

She told us that only days before her mother passed, her nephew called her mother (his grandmother) in the wee hours in the morning to talk with her. This wasn't just a one-time event but a regular occurrence. The truth was that her mother was always available for her children and grandchildren no matter the time. I thought, *I want to be this style of grandparent— available, approachable, and loving.* Did this mean I needed to make adjustments in my life? Yes, it did. Once a mom, always a mom (grandma).

Sweet friendships refresh the soul and awaken our hearts with joy, for good friends are like the anointing oil that yields the fragrant incense of God's presence.

PROVERBS 27:9 TPT

What adjustments will you need to make in your schedule to be available and approachable?

No matter whether you're nearing this season of parenting or you're a decade away from friendship with your kids, I want to encourage you, there is life after your children leave for college or their own apartment or home.

Look up Proverbs 27:9 and write what is sweet to a friendship.

I find this verse from *The Message* so encouraging: "Just as lotions and fragrance give sensual delight, a sweet friendship refreshes the soul." When our children become our friends, it can be one of the sweetest progressions of a relationship—one that may have been turbulent while raising them now turns enjoyable and refreshing.

Share a memory from your own experience growing up and becoming friends with your mom.

If friendship with your mom hasn't happened yet, don't be discouraged. Continue to reach out and make amends whenever possible.

There are lots of positive things about being good friends with your children. But it comes with a learning curve for sure. You want to be their friend, but not suffocate them with your presence. It's a hard balance, but one that needs to be established. I'm so thankful for the examples of my mother and mother-in-law that I've been able to glean from.

As a mom, enjoy friendship with your children, but allow them to have close friends outside your circle. Encourage their *other* friendships. And don't expect them to share everything with you. This will help keep your relationship healthy.

In what ways can you encourage your children's other friendships?

It seems as though kids go from toddlers to teens in a flash. Keep telling yourself, *Don't miss the captured moments along the way.* There seems to never be enough time to pour into your children the way you wish you could. And the desire to continue pouring into your grown kids doesn't end when they leave for college, move out, or get married. It's a full-time job that lasts a lifetime.

Even though my girls are now grown and on their own, I still want to be intentional with them. We never stop being a parent; it just looks different. We need to be creative and intentional as our kids leave the house.

On a winter's night, when my girls were young adults, I was awaiting the arrival of my daughters and ten of their friends for a mini house retreat. Many states would be represented, and joy filled my heart as I anticipated all of us gathering around my table to share stories and my pouring truth into the next generation. Moving into the friend zone is one of the greatest blessings. Live intentionally, and give life to your good intentions.

LET'S HEAR FROM OTHERS

Mickey shares ...

My mom has taught me everything I know about friendship. She has always had healthy relationships with other women. She is very intentional about making time for female friendships and has taught me to do the same. I have fond memories of my mom inviting me to run around with her and some of her friends. It was so special when she would let me tag along. Whether it was lunch, some retail therapy, or running errands, I didn't care. I just loved being with them! I didn't realize it then, but she was teaching me what true friendship looked like. I witnessed them serving, supporting, and encouraging one another, as well as celebrating and grieving with one another. I truly believe that observing her friendships taught me how to be a good friend and how to choose friends wisely.

At my bridal luncheon, several of my mom's dearest friends spoke, one by one, sharing memories of me growing up and speaking blessings over my marriage. You see, my mom wasn't the only one who was blessed by her friendships. I was blessed too, by growing up surrounded by amazing godly women and the developed friendship between me and my mom. I hope that some-day I'll be a good example to my children of what it means to be a good friend and that the people in my life will have a great influence on my children, just like my mom's friends have had on me!

ACTION STEP

Invite a few of your kids' friends over for a "just-because time" and enjoy being with them. Of course, the activity needs to be age-appropriate. It might be a dollar store activity or a pizza party.

PRAYER

Oh Lord, thank You for entrusting me with the children in my life and the privilege of being their mom. I dearly love them with all my heart and want them to grow up to be some of my very best friends. Guide the time I have with them as children and help me to release them to Your care and guidance as adults. You will fight for them and delight in them. Bless them and keep them. Let Your face shine upon them. In Your holy name, O God, I pray. Amen.

WRITE OUT YOUR THOUGHTS

WEEK FIVE

A legacy is something
that will follow you
but must be built
before we go.

KIM COLLINGSWORTH

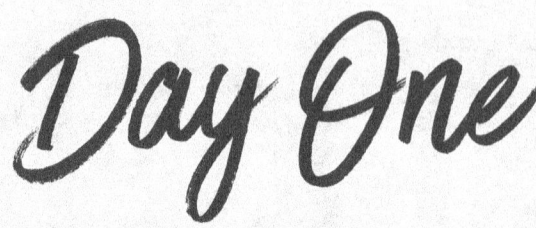

YOU GOT THIS!

But in all these things we overwhelmingly conquer through Him who loved us.

ROMANS 8:37

Okay, Mama, are you tired?

I know there may be days when you want to throw in the towel on this whole thing called motherhood. I certainly remember them all too well. Sometimes it was my own doing by trying to over-multitask and other days it was just the stress of trying to be the perfect parent. You may find yourself thinking things like *Don't these kids realize all I do for them? Don't they know how much I've sacrificed for them? When will they get it?*

Ugh. Some kids may realize at a young age all you've sacrificed for them, but others ... well, it may take until they have children of their own. I don't say this to heap discouragement on you, but so you'll realize you aren't alone.

Are you tired?

What are some things you do to reward yourself when you need to?

Look up Galatians 6:9–10 and write out what we aren't to weary in doing.

Remember this when your days are tough: There can be a seasonal time gap in the development of your children. There will be times when your kids may be delayed in appreciating all you do for them. I used to continually say to myself, *Many women have walked this road before me and made it. So can I.* And so can you, Mama.

As well, there will be situations when you may think your children's actions reflect your parenting skills. And again you heap the mama-guilt on yourself.

A dear friend, Lynne, shares her heart on how she finds balance between disappointment and unconditional love:

> First, I guess parenting and how your kid turns out are all in perspective. I remember sitting in a seminary class and the professor sharing how our children are made up of three parts: God's part, the parent's part, and the kid's part. All three of these parts build who our children become. If our children are successful, we can't take the glory and become too proud and puffed up, as it takes all three parts—God's part, the parent's part, and the kid's part. And if they don't live up to what we hoped or they go their own way, we can't take on the guilt and shame of their negative actions either, as it takes three parts for that particular decision—God's part, the parent's part, and the kid's part.

Share how the insight on how our children are made up of three parts encourages you.

Although our children ultimately make their choices, this doesn't mean we don't do our part as we are raising them. Some Christian parents misunderstand grace, calling for a "do-nothing policy" attitude toward discipline, but that is deadly. Discipline shows your children that there are consequences and accountability for sinful actions, and it demonstrates that there is a standard of right and wrong—one that they have fallen short of and thus need a Savior.

Our children are made up of three parts: God's part, the parent's part, and the kid's part.

Discipline is not simply rationing out punishment however we choose to carry it out under biblical guidelines. It's an opportunity for a gospel conversation where we tell our child that our love for them—and God's love for them—is not conditional based on their behavior, we confess that we're a sinner who has sinned in the exact same ways that they have, and we acknowledge that we need God's saving grace in Christ as much as they do.[40]

I know this seems over-spiritualizing at times. And that may be right.

There were many times when I just reacted without thinking it through; I gave a swift spanking and then talked afterwards. Then there were times when I said, "Go to your room and give me fifteen minutes to think this through." Yes, it was the best thing for them and for me.

Share what forms of discipline have worked for you.

This brings up another question—to spank or not to spank? The biblical approach to discipline and spanking is balanced, reasonable, and controlled. Our kids will feel most secure if they know we've set appropriate boundaries for them that we aren't afraid to enforce. They may not know they need boundaries, but oh they are screaming for them.

Look up Proverbs 3:11–12 and Proverbs 13:24 and write about how these Scriptures encourage you to discipline your children.

Some of the most intimate, touching moments you can have with your kids happen shortly after you've exercised discipline. So let me encourage you, after disciplining your child, take them in your arms and pray with them. This doesn't mean taking them out for ice cream to tell them you're sorry for disciplining them, but letting them know how thankful you are for them and that they're forgiven. Then give them a big hug and go do something positive with them. They'll know they're still accepted and that there's absolutely no barrier between the two of you.

There will also be times when you've mis-disciplined and you'll need to ask for your child's forgiveness. Never be afraid to say you're sorry if you were in the wrong. This will go so far, as your child sees your humanness and your own need for a Savior.

In the end, you're raising your child to be a respectable and responsible young adult. "Love, correct, guide, and sprinkle with more love" is a great equation for parenting your children.

Look up Proverbs 31:26 and write out what our instruction is to look like.

Look up Proverbs 3:3 and write out what we're to wear around our neck.

The part of Proverbs 31 that's made the biggest impact on me is verse 26: "When she speaks, her words are wise, and she gives instructions with kindness." There was a time while raising my girls when I felt like all I did was yell at them. I knew I didn't want them to grow up thinking I was a yeller. After reading this portion of Scripture, I sought the Lord and asked Him to search me and change me. I'm not saying I never raised my voice again or I didn't yell—okay, scream—at times. But I was certainly conscientious of how I spoke to them and tried to instruct them in a kinder manner. I sought to wear kindness as a necklace.

Is yelling part of your repertoire?

If yes, what steps will you take to be more kind in your instruction?

Let's finish this day with some practical areas where you can instruct your children.

First, look at your own life. Think about what's important to you and the lessons you've learned that you want to pass on to your children. Once you establish what's important to you, then teach that to your kids at the age-appropriate time. Most lessons will be ongoing, but some are by chance at the right moment. These God-ordained moments are something you can't plan for—they just happen—so be prepared the best you can. There are times you'll be caught off guard by something. If it's something you need to think on a little more, it's okay to tell your child, "I need to think on this and we will address it later." Just don't forget to address it.

Deliberately building into your children's lives helps young kids understand that outward behaviors are a picture of the inward relationship they have with Christ, and the importance of not just being hearers of the word but doers of the word (see James 1:22–23).

Practical Guidance to Pass Down to Your Children (Age-Appropriate)

1. BE TRUE TO WHO YOU ARE …
Help your child understand *whose* they are: "But as many as received Him, to them He gave the right to become children of God, even to those who believe in His name" (John 1:12 NASB).

2. USE GOOD COMMUNICATION SKILLS …
Help your child look others in the eye and speak directly to them. "A word fitly spoken is like apples of gold in a setting of silver" (Proverbs 25:11 ESV).

3. YOU ARE MORE THAN YOUR BODY …
Help your children understand that their bodies are not their own. Teach them about the importance of character, virtue, a royal priesthood, and holiness. "Or do you not know that your body is a temple of the Holy Spirit within you, whom you have from God? You are not your own, for you were bought with a price. So glorify God in your body" (1 Corinthians 6:19–20 ESV).

4. YOU HAVE CHOICES—SO CHOOSE WISELY …
Instruct your children that they have choices. Some of the choices will not be between what is good and bad, but what is good and best. "Become wise by walking with the wise; hang out with fools and watch your life fall to pieces" (Proverbs 13:20 MSG).

5. UNDERSTAND SOCIAL ETIQUETTE …
Teach your children how to act respectfully in public, from social media to respecting their elders. Decide how you will handle cell phones before handing one over to your child and set boundaries up-front. "So, as those who have been chosen of God, holy and beloved, put on a heart of compassion, kindness, humility, gentleness and patience; bearing with one another, and forgiving each other, whoever has a complaint against anyone; just as the Lord forgave you, so also should you. Beyond all these things put on love, which is the perfect bond of unity" (Colossians 3:12–14 NASB)

6. HAVE TABLE MANNERS …
Teach your child proper etiquette around the table. Don't forget the importance of eating together. Make a conscious effort to have dinner as a family. "Let your speech always be gracious, seasoned with salt, so that you may know how you ought to answer each person" (Colossians 4:12 ESV).

7. UNDERSTAND HOME ECONOMICS …
Include your children when you're folding laundry, cleaning, cooking, gardening, and more. Teach them basic home-keeping skills. It may take you a little longer to

get things done, but you'll be raising them up to care for their own home one day. "Older men are to be temperate, dignified, self-controlled, sound in faith, in love, and in endurance. Older women likewise are to exhibit behavior fitting for those who are holy, not slandering, not slaves to excessive drinking, but teaching what is good. In this way they will train the younger women to love their husbands, to love their children, to be self-controlled, pure, fulfilling their duties at home, kind, being subject to their own husbands, so that the message of God may not be discredited" (Titus 2:2–5 NET).

8. BE THANKFUL ...
Train your children to have a spirit of thankfulness. Teach them to write thank-you notes or send a text letting a gift giver know they received their gift. Acknowledging the person giving a gift, their time, or themselves is respectful. It's a lost art in today's society, but you can bring it back. It'll help your children become more grateful for the big and small gestures. "I have not stopped giving thanks for you, or remembering you in my prayers" (Ephesians 1:16 NIV).

9. PRACTICE MODESTY ...
Instruct your children in the quality of not being too proud or confident about themselves or their abilities. And teach them the state of being proper or suitable. Of course this one is age-appropriate when addressing their attire, but it can never be taught too early. Modesty is the first line of defense for purity.[41] "Likewise the women are to dress in suitable apparel, with modesty and self-control. Their adornment must not be with braided hair and gold or pearls or expensive clothing, but with good deeds, as is proper for women who profess reverence for God" (1 Timothy 2:9–10 NET).

10. NAVIGATE FRIENDSHIPS WISELY ...
Encourage your children to choose their friends wisely. You'll want their closest friends to be like-minded. Be careful with whom you allow your children to spend time. "As iron sharpens iron, so a person sharpens his friend" (Proverbs 27:17 NET).

11. HANDLE SEX AND PUBERTY CAREFULLY ...
Sexuality is at the core of our human existence. Therefore, we have a responsibility to equip our children with a comprehensive view of sexuality taught within the context of a biblically holistic approach. As for timing and when to get started,

there's no time like the present. No two children are alike, even in the same family. You'll want to be sensitive to how your children are developing physically, mentally, emotionally, and spiritually. You also want sex education to occur in both spontaneous and structured moments.[42]

To be honest with you, after talking with many women, I've learned that discussions regarding sex is the area of greatest regret while raising their kids. So learn from us— start earlier rather than later. Don't only share the bad side of sex, but the beautiful side within the confines of marriage between a woman and a man. "Oh, let me warn you, sisters in Jerusalem, by the gazelles, yes, by all the wild deer: Don't excite love, don't stir it up, until the time is ripe—and you're ready" (Song of Solomon 3:5 MSG).

Please know this is not an exhaustive list, but it's a good start for passing biblical principles and practical tips down to your children.

What are some things you would like to pass down to your children in your current season of parenting?

LET'S HEAR FROM OTHERS

Melissa shares ...

I didn't want to wait for my daughters to be a certain age and have one big talk on sex. It just seemed awkward. So I decided to have an open conversation on a need-to-know basis. Their questions were answered simply in an honest and direct way based on their maturity level. I tried to keep movies and TV kid-friendly, and was pretty strict about what they read.

It became messy when a single woman we knew became pregnant. My youngest looked up at me and said, "Mom, I thought people had to be married so the baby has a mom and a dad." It made me so sad to see how her innocence was being lost. So I asked for advice on books, picked out the best one, and taught her basic biology.

Society and our culture had caught me off guard. From that point on, I looked for teachable moments and tried to keep the conversation going. When a popular book series for young people included a vampire romance, I read it with my daughter and we talked about exclusive dating and its effects. I tried to keep up with what they heard through media and in school and continue the conversation. The goal was to try to keep them talking.

 **ACTION STEP**

This week, choose an area you wish to address and take a step to pass down a biblical principle to your children.

PRAYER

Oh Lord, I praise You that You are the perfect Father and that all Your ways are pure. Help me tap into Your power and wisdom when I don't know how to handle a particular situation.

I lay my children at Your feet and pray that they'll have a desire to please You above everyone else and all things.

May they truly know Your love for themselves. In Your holy name, O God, I pray. Amen.

WRITE OUT YOUR THOUGHTS

GOD'S GROWTH CHART

And Jesus increased in wisdom and stature,
and in favor with God and man.

LUKE 2:52

Today, I want to practically look at character traits we want to build into our kids and give you a plumb line for growth that you'll want to see increase as your children mature.

Look up 1 Chronicles 28:9 and write out the important instruction David wanted to instill into his son Solomon.

Know, serve, seek, and find—these are the things we want to instill in our kids as they grow, and then hopefully they'll embrace them as they mature. They may not be things the world would consider worth seeking after, but in God's eyes, they're important and they're what will last for eternity.

Look up Philippians 4:8–9 and write down the things we should think on.

Look up 2 Peter 1:5–10 and write down the Christian qualities listed.

These are not just a list of good qualities, but ones we are to practice in our everyday lives. Both portions of Scripture tell us to practice these qualities. They are a good plumb line for us and for our kids. We'll want our kids to see us living out these qualities in our own lives as well. As your children grow physically, it's equally important to see the qualities listed be evident in their lives as they mature spiritually. The way they think will dictate their lives. You'll want to see the things in Philippians 4:8 move from a thought to an action as they practice them.

How do you see your children maturing in these qualities? (This will vary with the age of your children, but you can still observe areas or growth at any age.)

Two of our end goals as parents are to help our children become responsible young adults and to work ourselves out of a job. This doesn't mean we won't continue to guide them, but it's part of the *de*-parenting process of not always figuring everything out for them.

One of the hardest things for me while raising my girls was allowing them to fail—not fixing every heartache, discouragement, and disappointment. Oh yes, you'll be there for moral support, a hug, and a shoulder to cry on, but there will be things you won't be able to fix and your child will have to walk through less-than-perfect situations. This is where the growth chart from Philippians and 2 Peter will be visible as they mature. It'll become part of their story. Both success and failure build into the destiny of the person they'll become.

For the remainder of this day, I want us to focus on one verse that has big meaning and explains the roles of sons and daughters.[43] The first time I studied this Scripture, it made a great impact on my life. I hope it will do the same for you.

Look up Psalm 144:12 and write down what it says about the character of sons and daughters.

Explain in your own words what you think this verse says.

Here's what Psalm 144:12 says about sons in the different versions:

- "Let our sons in their youth be as grown-up plants" (NASB).
- "May our sons flourish in their youth like well-nurtured plants" (MSG).
- "Then our sons in their youth will be like well-nurtured plants" (NIV).

The trees represented in Psalm 144:12 are "well-nurtured." They're not trees growing in the wild, but rather trees planted by hand in a location specially chosen to produce the best growth. They are well cared for so that they'll grow to maturity at an early age. They have deep roots in good soil. This is a picture of young men in their growing-up years becoming strong and powerful, like a forest of mighty oak trees.

What does a young man like this look like?

- There is nothing shameful about him.
- He stands strong and tall and clean and pure.

- He has a strong character, and others come to him for shade and to find safety.
- His thoughts are pure.
- His actions are noble.
- His intentions point in the right direction.

Here's what Psalm 144:12 says about daughters in the different versions:

- "And our daughters as corner pillars fashioned as for a palace" (NASB).
- "May our daughters be like graceful pillars carved to beautify a palace" (NET).
- "And our daughters will be like pillars carved to adorn a palace" (NIV).

In Bible times, beautiful palaces contained multiple large columns that were both decorative and weight-bearing. The most expensive columns were cut from marble, highly polished, and carefully put in place. The most important of those columns were placed at the intersection of two or more walls. They united various parts of the building, connecting one wing with another.

Those corner columns were crucial because they held everything together. The master craftsmen would take extra time, choosing the best materials and working overtime to produce stone cut to exacting measurements and polished to a high degree of brilliance. The corner columns were placed with exquisite care because the integrity of the entire building depended on them. If they were cut wrong or placed incorrectly, the entire building would be unsound. But when properly placed, they became the foundation and connecting point for everything else.

> Let our sons in their youth be as grown-up plants, and our daughters as corner pillars fashioned as for a palace.
>
> PSALM 144:12

Don't be deceived by the emphasis on beauty and grace. These columns are not mere ornaments added to please the eye. They are the corner pillars that hold the palace together.

What does a young woman like this look like?

- They are like those highly polished, carefully chosen, perfectly placed corner columns that hold together the palace where the king dwells.

- There is both form and function.
- They are both beautiful and strong.
- They hold the family together and serve as the connecting point for everything else.
- They are at the center of family life.
- Everything flows to them and through them.[44]

Please understand that sons like this do not happen by accident any more than a beautiful garden plants itself, waters itself, weeds itself, and fertilizes itself. Nor do daughters like this happen by accident. There is no clumsy workmanship here. Only a master craftsman can produce beautiful corner columns fit for a king's palace.

Do you dream of these things for your sons and daughters?

Here's a prayer for your son:

Oh Lord, I pray, that my son(s) _____,
at an early age, would be firmly rooted in the good soil of your Word—that his roots might be so strong and so deep in the Word that he can stand strong in every storm. In Jesus's name, amen.

Here's a prayer for your daughter:

Oh Lord, I pray, that my daughter(s) _____,
would know her worth from an early age and that she would grow to reflect the beauty of the Lord in all she does. I pray that she would remain close to our family and be a contributing part of the cohesiveness of our family dynamics as she matures into adulthood. In Jesus's name, amen.

LET'S HEAR FROM OTHERS

Sandy shares ...

When my girls were really little, God awakened my spirit to the reality that Satan wanted them. It didn't matter their age, from the time they were born he was pursuing them. This was a harsh reality for me to swallow, but I knew that just like God pursues them because He loves them, Satan pursues them because he hates them. I realized that a big part of my responsibility as a mother was to fight on their behalf.

As I watched them grow and discover life—even in the early learning stages—I would notice ways that Satan was targeting them (anger, fear, and anxiety, to name a few). I began to battle on my knees, praying Scripture over their lives and declaring out loud that they belonged to God. A big part of raising children who are pillars and trees in the kingdom of God, is armoring up, going to war with the enemy of their soul, and engaging in the battle at every stage of their lives.

ACTION STEP

Make a point to acknowledge the growth you see in your children and personally encourage them.

PRAYER

Oh Lord, help us as parents to live so that our children find it easy to believe in Jesus. Give us children of strong faith who are not ashamed to live for Christ. We ask for a single-minded focus on things of eternal value. May we say, "But as for me and my house, we will serve the Lord" (Joshua 24:15). In Your holy name, O God, I pray. Amen.

WRITE OUT YOUR THOUGHTS

Day Three

DANDELION FAITH

I have no greater joy than this, to hear of my children walking in the truth.

3 JOHN 1:4

One summer day while I was watching my grandson, we were outside playing. Dandelion season was in full bloom, and as we looked over the field where we were playing, there was one dandelion after another. When we were through with a good time at the park, we sat on our picnic blanket eating lunch and I explained to him the game you play by blowing on the dandelion. I proceeded to show him as you puff on the whimsical flower, you make a wish on something you want to see happen in the future. It's not a sure thing that this wish will come to pass, but it's a fun thing to do. His wish that day was, "I wish, I wish, I wish I lived with Mimi forever."

I share this cute story to make a very important point: This doesn't just have to be a wish; it can be the reality of eternity.

Read 1 Thessalonians 4:15–18 and write about the progression of believers.

I love the last part of 1 Thessalonians 4:17: "and so we shall always be with the Lord." Yes, you and your loved ones can live for all eternity together. Your responsibilities as a parent are to talk with your children about the Lord in your home, to be a good steward of bringing them to church regularly, and to expose them to biblical truths as much as possible.

Before we move forward, I want to make sure your walk with God is secure—that you're taking care of yourself. Remember the analogy of the oxygen mask from the first day? Well, this is the biggest and most important part of taking care of yourself first!

Look up John 3:15–18 and write down what it says about eternal life.

Have you accepted that Jesus is the one and only Son of God and that He died for the forgiveness of your sins?

If yes, briefly share your testimony.

If no, please see "Christ in Your Heart" on page 209 for the steps to secure your eternal security and please tell someone in your group.

Okay, now let's move on to your children …

I'm sure you have high aspirations for your kids. Maybe you dream of them becoming a doctor one day, or a professional athlete or the next person to find a cure. These ambitions are not bad in and of themselves. And of course, no matter what your children become, you hope they enjoy what they do. However, if you fail to have a yearning for their spiritual life, you're missing the greatest joy and highest accomplishment as a parent.

Look up Proverbs 4:20–27 and answer the following questions.

Who is this portion of Scripture directed to (v. 20)?

Who do these words come from (v. 20)?

What is their instruction (v. 21)?

What is the result of your children listening (v. 22)?

What should you guard (v. 23)?

Where should your gaze be (vv. 25–27)?

As I pondered this portion of Scripture myself, I looked in the column of my Bible and saw the names of my grandchildren written there. Yes, this should be the highest desire for you and your children and the next generation—to love the Lord with all their heart, walk in His ways, and *not* to turn away from the truths of God.

Look up 3 John 1–4 and write down the greatest joy of a parent.

From this verse, we see the joy John experiences knowing that his fellow companion, Gaius, whom John probably led to Christ, was walking in truth. This is the same joy we experience when our children come to a saving knowledge of Christ and are walking in His truths.

So, now that we have the desires of our heart intact, eternity can seem like it's a long ways away, can't it? However, it's just like raising our children. It seems like if we blink, we'll miss it. Yes, it will come fast. But one of the blessings of living under the rule of Christ is that you can experience a piece of heaven in the here and now.

Look up the following verses and match them to the gift of the here and now.

Psalm 27:13   **I will see the goodness of the Lord in the land of the living.**

Psalm 116:9   **The Word (Jesus) came down from above to live among us.**

John 1:14   **And so I walk in the Lord's presence as I live here on earth.**

Yes, you and I can experience the goodness of God while living in this crazy world. Will it take effort on our part? Absolutely. We'll need to be intentional (there's that word again) to bring heaven's presence down into our everyday life.

So, how do we do this? By doing all the things we've already discussed through this study—seeking God daily, watching for blessings from God, and inviting him into our everyday life—make the reality of Christ a part of our coming and going.

> I have no greater joy than this, to hear of my children walking in the truth.
>
> 3 JOHN 4

When we allow the love of God to be poured into our heart through the Holy Spirit who was given to us (see Romans 5:5), in turn we'll be able to love others. Being firmly rooted and built up in Him and established in our faith, we overflow with gratitude (see Colossians 2:7), and since we've been raised up with Christ, we keep seeking the things above, where Christ is seated at the right hand of God, and setting our mind on the things above, not on the things that are on earth (see Colossians 3:1–2).

When we do this, we'll be able to look at our children through a different lens. This little acrostic for LOVE can change the way we see and parent our children.

L ove

O thers in

V iew of

E ternity

I know it's not always easy to love others in view of eternity and it takes time to get over particular situations, but it will be beneficial for us to keep a steadfast mind on things from above.

In Colossians 3:2, Paul tells us, "Set your minds on things above, not on the things that are on the earth." As we close this day, let's take a glimpse into what the apostle John observed when he was given his vision of heaven.

Read Revelation 4:1–11. What is God worthy of (v. 11)?

In awe of the greatness of God, let's think about His greatness daily as we live for Him—here and now. May our lives produce the "things above," such as compassion, kindness, humility, gentleness, patience, forgiveness, and love (see Colossians 3:12–14), as we parent our children.

Setting our minds on things above doesn't mean that we should live in a mystical fog or neglect our affairs in the here and now. What it does mean is that we're not only to be concerned with the trivialities of the temporal, but that we should also view everything (actions and relationships) against the backdrop of eternity. With this new perspective on life, the eternal will surely have an impact on the temporal.[45] That means we do even the mundane things, like cooking dinner, cleaning the house, and reading the same book over and over, with a better attitude. Oh boy, does that hit home!

Mama, you're doing great! We only have two more days. Let's finish strong!

LET'S HEAR FROM OTHERS

Carolyn, describing her real-mom solution to keeping a heavenly perspective while rearing children in the here and now, says ...

While rearing seven children—one with a strong will, one with developmental disabilities, three with complex early childhood trauma, and the remaining two typically developing (which is challenging enough)—I had many times when I needed to confess for lack of patience, kindness, gentleness, etc. And not just to God, but to my kids. Herein lies a gift I gave and continue to give my children, my grandchildren, and myself—humility flowing from a broken and contrite heart before God and them. They continue to witness my faith in action, our loving God who welcomes and forgives, and a mother who needs Jesus every day ... minute by minute.

ACTION STEP

Have fun and play a silly game with your kids. If it's dandelion season, make a wish.

PRAYER

Oh Lord, I pray that my children will develop an eternal perspective with wisdom and purpose that comes from You, not from this world. Help them to see life—and every challenge—through Your eyes. I pray that they'll set their mind on things above, not just on the here and now, and that they'll be rooted and grounded in Your love. May they be filled with You from morning till night. In Your holy name, O God, I pray. Amen.

WRITE OUT YOUR THOUGHTS

Day Four

HIGH-LOW-BUFFALO

Now to Him who is able to do far more abundantly beyond all that we ask or think,
according to the power that works within us.

EPHESIANS 3:20

Hey Mama, we're going to have some fun today, and I hope this little exercise becomes part of your every day! Today's work comes from my book *High, Low, Buffalo: The Power of God-Centered Perspective.*

As you reflect on the close of each day and consider the day's findings, you may wonder if anything you did made an impact on your family and moved you forward. Some days, you may find yourself in the same rut as the day before. It begs the question, do you need to make a change or just view life through a different lens? This is where *High-Low-Buffalo* comes in—it's time to refresh your perspective. And I sure hope working through this study has done just that.

Whether my family is together for a day or an extended period of time, my daughter Sarah challenges us to share a *high-low-buffalo.* The *high* represents the exciting and best part of your day, while the *low* represents a disappointment or less-than-desirable experience. The final part is the *buffalo,* or that random, unexpected blessing you experienced—a welcome surprise.

This is a fun and reflective way to close out your day, but deciding what to share takes a good bit of consideration and intentionality. What you choose to be your high-low-buffalo is all determined by the perspective you choose to have as you reflect on your day.

Perspective is so important. Positivity defers you from thoughts that send you into a downward spiral. It provides a strong mindset to override the negative talk you tell yourself. A positive Christian is a contagious Christian—one who draws deep joy from Christ and in turn draws others to Him.

You've heard it said a million times—okay, maybe not a million times, but a lot—that perspective is everything. Change your perspective, and you may be able to change your life.

Write out Proverbs 23:7 and what it means to you.

What you and I think, will dictate our actions. What we dwell on will be a plumb line for processing a situation. Too many times our perspective is altered by what we think we should do, who we should be, or how we should act. The "Mama should ..." mindset leads to disappointment most times. Avoiding this perception will result in a happier life. Not a perfect life, but one grounded in the truths of who you are in Christ.

Changing your inner self-talk can change the way you carry yourself, feel about yourself, and view the world around you. If you replace negative talk with positive truth, God will guard your heart and mind with what He thinks about you.

Is there something you think about yourself that needs to change?

Do you battle "Mama should …" guilt?

Right thinking begins with the words you speak to yourself and where your thoughts are fixed—on what is true, honorable, right, pure, lovely, admirable, excellent, and worthy of praise. It's time to stop the cycle of wrong thinking, and start dwelling on the truths of God and allow His promise of peace to wash over your mind.

Let's practice the exercise of High-Low-Buffalo …

What's been your high while working through this study?

What's been your high in motherhood?

If any, what's been your low while working through this study?

What's been your low in motherhood?

What's been your buffalo while working through this study?

What's been your buffalo in motherhood?

Look up Ephesians 5:15–16 and write out what you're to make the most of.

Our highs can be defining moments if we embrace them as *kairos* moments. Ephesians 5:15–16 encourages us, "Therefore be careful how you walk, not as unwise men but as wise, making the most of *your time*, because the days are evil."

Time can be categorized as *chronos*, which is sequential—past, present, future. And it is linear, moving in only one direction. This is how humans measure time, but God exists outside the space-time dimensions He created.

Another word for *time* is *kairos*, which refers to the opportune time that characterizes Ephesians 5:16. Chronos counts minutes. Kairos captures moments. It's the critical moment or the appointed time—"for such a time as this" (Esther 4:14). It's carpe diem, "seize the day."[46]

Do you find it difficult some days to "seize the day"?

Seize the moment.

Between your "Once upon a time …" and your "… happily ever after" is your *now*. Don't miss the opportunity to instill biblical principles into your children. No matter how busy you might think you are, you'll always need to make the time to be there for your family, no matter how old your children are. Yes, there will be times when you're not able to be at an event, answer a phone call, or be the taxi. But make sure this isn't the norm and is just an occasional occurrence.

Seizing the day will take great intentionality. It'll require you to be where your feet are, from the grocery-store visit to a well-planned vacation and everything in between. It's about being aware of your surroundings and capitalizing on the moments you're given because you never get that time back.

Never stop tucking your kids into bed!

Ugh. I know what you may be thinking: *Boy, have I blown it*. Don't be so hard on yourself! I've missed one too many opportunities too. I think we all have. But we can move forward, watching for opportune times and embracing the ordinary moments with a fresh intent to make a difference in the lives of people God sends our way. It may mean a slower pace of life, a more watchful eye, or having a different focused outlook. Whatever it is, embrace the moment and thank God for another chance to make a difference in your life and the lives of your children.

Your days' highs will be the highlights of your focus and in turn produce a grateful heart. Then there's the lows. We all have them. But does it mean we have to like them? If we're honest, we'd rather not experience them. However, we must come to a place where we hit our nemesis head-on and accept lows for what they are—a less-than-desirable situation. And while it may not seem like it at first, something positive can come from the experience and become your greatest buffalo. Often, when we reach deeper into the situation, there's a wider lesson learned through our lows; it comes from the comfort we receive from God as He gently cares for us and walks beside us through our unwelcome circumstance.

Look up Deuteronomy 6:4–7 one more time and write out when you are to talk with your kids about the Lord.

I love these verses because they give validity to one of the most important things we can do with and for our children: *Never stop tucking your kids into bed!* Yup—don't stop tucking them into bed, no matter their ages. While doing this, you'll experience many highs, a few lows, and a lot of buffaloes.

I know there may be nights you'll want to skip this part of your routine (and you will), but don't allow it to become the norm. Something special happens in the dark of the night while the moonlight streams through your child's bedroom window. They're more likely to share things with you that they won't share in the light of the day, and you won't want to miss this opportunity into the window of their soul.

When our girls returned home from college over a break or for the summer, I kept up this nightly ritual. But this season of life brought some changes and our girls started to tuck us in! John and

I started to go to bed before them, and they would sit at the foot of our bed talking over the day. And now even after they've become mothers, when they spend the night at our house, we sit on our beds going over our high-low-buffaloes of the day.

Do you tuck your children into bed?

If not, will you start to make it a regular practice?

LET'S HEAR FROM OTHERS

My dear friend Tami is the mother of five boys from ages thirteen to thirty. She has great things to say about her own mom ...

Some of my best memories are of my mom making fudge jumbles (high) for me and my friends who would come over on the weekend and sit around the kitchen island eating and laughing. My friends loved coming to our house because there was always fun food, good conversation, Ping Pong, go-karts, ATVs, motorcycles, and more (lots of buffaloes). My mom made me want to be home and bring my friends with me, and all these years later, my boys find their grandma's home a safe haven too.

 **ACTION STEP**

If you haven't tucked your children into bed recently, don't miss another night.

PRAYER

Oh Lord, I am so thankful for the times we celebrate the great highs in our life, learn from the lows, and enjoy the buffaloes. Help us as a family to view life from Your perspective and see our days as a gift from You. In Your holy name, O God, I pray. Amen.

WRITE OUT YOUR THOUGHTS

Day Five

THE TOP TEN THINGS I WISH I'D KNOWN AS A YOUNG MOTHER

Whatever you do, do your work heartily, as for the Lord rather than for men.

COLOSSIANS 3:23

Well, here we are, the last day of the study! You did it, Mama! Great job. You can add a star to your chart. All kidding aside, you've worked very hard. I hope you have been blessed by this study and will continue to walk out this thing called motherhood with stronger endurance, resilience beyond your own strength, and a deeper love for God and family.

Are you going to make mistakes? Of course! But in those times you're going to encounter El Roi, the God who sees—the God who loves you and is watching over you.

I want to take this last day to share with you the top ten things I wish I'd known as a young mom. These will be a reminder and a recap of all that we've talked about and an encouragement to you as we end this study.

1. **Enjoy a close walk with God through the busyness of motherhood.**

   "Enoch was sixty-five years old when his son Methuselah was born. Afterwards he lived another 300 years in fellowship with God, and produced sons and daughters; then, when he was 365, and in constant touch with God, he disappeared, for God took him!" (Genesis 5:21–24 TLB).

   How has this study encouraged you to enjoy your walk with God?

   What do you need to do to prioritize this principle?

2. **Have a marriage-centered home, not a child-centered home.**

   "What therefore God has joined together, let no man separate" (Mark 10:9).

   If you're married, how has this study encouraged you to put your marriage before your kids?

   What do you need to do to prioritize this principle?

3. **Watch for teachable moments.**

   "Give instruction to a wise man and he will be still wiser, teach a righteous man and he will increase his learning" (Proverbs 9:9).

   How has this study encouraged you to be more aware of watching for teachable moments?

What do you need to do to prioritize this principle?

4. Embrace sacrifice as an obedience to God and not a hindrance.

"Whatever you do, do your work heartily, as for the Lord rather than for men" *(Colossians 3:23).*

How has this study encouraged you to embrace sacrifice?

What do you need to do to prioritize this principle?

5. Allow others to help.

"Two are better than one because they have a good return for their labor" *(Ecclesiastes 4:9).*

How has this study encouraged you to allow others into your children's lives?

What do you need to do to prioritize this principle?

6. Create one-on-one time for your husband and children no matter their age.

"Just as you know how we were exhorting and encouraging and imploring each one of you as a father would his own children, so that you would walk in a manner worthy of the God who calls you into His own kingdom and glory" *(1 Thessalonians 2:11–12).*

How has this study encouraged you to be more intentional with creating memories?

What do you need to do to prioritize this principle?

7. **Love your children in view of eternity.**

"If then you have been raised with Christ, seek the things that are above, where Christ is, seated at the right hand of God. Set your minds on things that are above, not on things that are on earth" (Colossians 3:1–3).

How has this study encouraged your parenting with an eternal-purpose mentality?

What do you need to do to prioritize this principle?

8. **Seize the moment and be present in the now.**

"So teach us to number our days, that we may present to You a heart of wisdom" (Psalm 90:12).

How has this study encouraged you to appreciate each season of motherhood?

What do you need to do to prioritize this principle?

9. **Friendship with your children is not for during the rearing stage.**

   "He who withholds his rod hates his son, but he who loves him disciplines him diligently" (Proverbs 13:24).

   How has this study encouraged you to understand the importance of friendship with your children?

   What do you need to do to prioritize this principle?

10. **Never stop tucking your kids into bed.**

    "You shall teach them diligently to your sons and shall talk of them when you sit in your house and when you walk by the way and when you lie down and when you rise up" (Deuteronomy 6:7).

    How has this study encouraged you to finish out your day with your children?

    What do you need to do to prioritize this principle?

Raising your children is an ongoing process that purifies you and develops them through countless hours on your knees. May God continue to show you ways to raise your children as you meet daily with Him in the quietness of your spirit.

Let me further encourage you with an example from Susannah Wesley. Susannah was the mother of nineteen children, including John and Charles Wesley, the founders of Methodism. She made following God and prayer a priority.

Because she had so many children who she reared, educated, and taught the fear of the Lord to, she at times found it difficult to find quiet time for herself. One of the most dramatic examples of how busy and crowded the house often was is that as a signal to her children to be quiet, Susannah would sometimes sit down and pull her apron over her head so she could pray in peace. When she was thus accoutred, the children knew not to interrupt her.[47]

Basically, in today's words, "Shush! Leave Mom alone!" So whether your kids are babies, tweens, or getting ready to leave the nest, exemplify a quiet example of your personal relationship with your heavenly Father and where God fits into the equation. At times, no words need to be spoken. The actions speak volumes.

Because of Susannah's example and strong influence, John Wesley was one of the movers and shakers in his generation who impacted the Christian world with his most famous aphorisms: "Do all the good you can, by all the means you can, in all the ways you can, in all the places you can, at all the times you can, to all the people you can, as long as ever you can."

Be a woman who raises your children with great intentionality. Have grit to keep going, and don't forget to wear kindness as a necklace. Oh, Mama, you be the difference!

LET'S HEAR FROM OTHERS

Verna shares a beautiful remembrance with us ...

I sometimes wonder if my mother could be the same parent today as she was in the 50s. Although the voices of culture have made radical changes in family life, I believe she could. Her child-rearing principles were unchanging. Challenges are countless for the moms of today. I speak with many women who are weary-busy.

I understand. I remember.

Oh, but the challenges of yesteryear moms must have seemed overwhelming. Think about the ancient moms of the Bible. The garden mom, Eve, the first woman to have a baby—wow! No books, no midwife. After the fall, she suffered the heartbreak of dysfunction in her family ... brother against brother. The sacred mama of Jesus labored while on a donkey, birthing her holy baby on the floor of a cave. And then, this young mom had the responsibility to teach and protect the baby Messiah. Fast-forward to the time of television moms, extremes from June Cleaver to Peg Bundy, the "ladies we've learned from." However, my admiration was for Caroline Ingalls, the wise and patient pioneer mom of *Little House on the Prairie*.

She never had a meltdown.

Through the ages, God's design for the amazing role of mother-dom is unchanging ... to give life, teach, nurture and protect the heritage He has given us. It has been my privilege to be a mom, no matter the stage my children were *growing through*, no matter the season I was *going through*. I have learned much from them.

And, unlike Ma Ingalls, I've had a meltdown ...

No matter how our culture changes, a mother's heart remains.

I look to my own mom, an everlasting example to me ... not a biblical mom, not a TV mom, but a practical woman with extravagant dedication to her family. Her eye was faithfully upon me clear and steady, and remained upon me even when it became faded and

framed with flesh timelines—still holding out a wrinkled hand of help. She infused and handed down strength into her great-grand-daughters. No matter what stage of mama-hood or gramma-hood, we can be a strong influence and example to leave long after our home-going.[48]

ACTION STEP

Choose one of the ten top things I wish I'd known as a young mom and implement the principle into your week.

PRAYER

Oh Lord God, may my children not fear, for You are with them. As I place my children in Your mighty, loving hands, give me peace, knowing that You are right by their side. Please replace their fears with the strength and courage to face whatever the day brings. Give my children a real sense that Jesus is with them. In Your holy name, O God, I pray. Amen.

WRITE OUT YOUR THOUGHTS

CHRIST IN YOUR HEART

Are you in this study wondering how you can ask Jesus into your heart and what *born again* means? In the New Testament book of John, Jesus had a conversation with a man named Nicodemus who approached Him, curious about the kingdom of God. Jesus told Nicodemus, "I tell you the truth, unless you are born again, you cannot see the Kingdom of God" (John 3:3 NLT).

In the next verse Nicodemus responded, "How can an old man go back into his mother's womb and be born again?" As a respected leader in the Jewish community, Nicodemus was a moral man who obeyed God's law. But even though he was a fine man, something was lacking from his life.

Like Nicodemus, many people today confuse "being good" with a real new-birth experience. New birth begins when the Holy Spirit convicts a person of sin. Because of the fall of man (Genesis 3), we are spiritually dead and in need of a Savior. God so loves us that He gives us spiritual birth when we ask Him for it.

The Bible says all persons are sinners (Romans 3:23). Jesus, God's Son, died on a cross and was raised from the dead to save sinners (Colossians 1:20), and we are told that if we believe in the Lord Jesus, we will be saved (Acts 16:31). To be born again means that a person admits to God that he or she is a sinner, repents of their sin (Acts 3:19), believes and trusts in Jesus Christ, and confesses faith in Christ as Savior (John 1:12).

Jesus told Nicodemus that every person who believes in Christ would not perish (John 3:16). Jesus is the only One who can save us (John 14:6). To believe in Jesus is to be born anew.

Take this moment to confess your sins and ask Jesus to save you, and Christ will live in your heart. Please don't put off this important decision. Acts 2:21 tells us, "For anyone who calls on the name of the Lord will be saved." Upon receiving Jesus Christ into your heart, share this important decision with another person—maybe your Bible study leader, your spouse, or a dear friend. I pray that you will find a Bible-believing church to attend so you can continue to worship God, grow in Christ, and serve in the Spirit.

Dear Mama, this is a day to rejoice and be happy. Congratulations!

ADDITIONAL RESOURCES

- *31 Days to Becoming a Happy Mom* by Arlene Pellicane
- *936 Pennies: Discovering the Joy of Intentional Parenting* by Eryn Lynum
- *Becoming Mom Strong* by Heidi St. John
- *Brave Bible Study* by Tabitha Deller
- *Calm, Cool, and Connected: 5 Digital Habits for a More Balanced Life* by Arlene Pellicane
- *Gathering Seeds of Encouragement* by Verna Bowman
- *Growing Up Social: Raising Relational Kids in a Screen-Driven World* by Gary Chapman and Arlene Pellicane
- *Moms Raising Sons to Be Men: Guiding Them Toward Their Purpose and Passion* by Rhonda Stoppe
- *Parents Rising: 8 Strategies for Raising Kids Who Love God, Respect Authority, and Value What's Right* by Arlene Pellicane
- *Quieting the Shout of Should: How a Life of Less Can Lead to More* by Crystal Stine
- *Raising Girls: Diaper to Diamond* by Jessie Seneca
- *Room of a Mother's Heart: A Sacred Call and an Eternal Purpose* by Carol McLeod
- *Rooted in Wonder: Nurturing Your Family's Faith Through God's Creation* by Eryn Lynum
- *Screen Kids: 5 Relational Skills Every Child Needs in a Tech-Driven World* by Gary Chapman and Arlene Pellicane
- *The New Strong-Willed Child* By Dr. James C. Dobson

ENDNOTES

1. Oswald Chambers, *My Utmost for His Highest* (Nashville: Thomas Nelson, 1993), November 28 reading.

2. "Resilience," Wikipedia, https://en.wikipedia.org/w/index.php?title=Resilience.

3. "H2428 — ḥayil — Strong's Hebrew Lexicon (CSB)," Blue Letter Bible, https://www.blueletterbible.org/lexicon/h2428/csb/wlc/0-1/.

4. Gary Martin, "'Pull Yourself up by Your Bootstraps' – The Meaning and Origin of This Phrase," Phrasefinder, www.phrases.org.uk/meanings/pull-yourself-up-by-your-bootstraps.html.

5. Chambers, *My Utmost for His Highest*, August 2 reading.

6. Catherine Chen, Ph.D., "The Difference Between Perfection and a Healthy Pursuit of Excellence," *The Huffington Post*, August 24, 2013, https://www.huffpost.com/entry/the-difference-between-perfection_b_3490442.

7. Marc Winn, "Perfectionism vs. Excellence," The View Inside Me, February 27, 2013, https://theviewinside.me/perfectionism-vs-excellence/.

8. "H2428 — hayil — Strong's Hebrew Lexicon (CSB)," Blue Letter Bible, https://www.blueletterbible.org/lexicon/h2428/csb/wlc/0-1/.

9. "G3306 — menō – Strong's Greek Lexicon (KJV)," Blue Letter Bible, https://www.blueletterbible.org/lexicon/g3306/kjv/tr/0-1/.

10. *Merriam-Webster.com Dictionary*, s.v. "-ing," https://www.merriam-webster.com/dictionary/-ing.

11. "When Friendship Fades," Blogs by J, April 16, 2020, https://blogbyj.life/2020/04/16/when-friendship-fades/.

12. Laura Lifshitz, "The Other Woman Who Snuggles My Daughter," *The New York Times*, December 27, 2015, https://archive.nytimes.com/parenting.blogs.nytimes.com/2015/12/27/the-other-woman-who-snuggles-my-daughter/.

13. Kevin Kabel, "Proverbs 3:27–28," Calvary Heights Baptist Church, June 19, 2019, calvaryheightsbc.com/blog/2019/06/19/proverbs-3-27-28.

14. J. Lee Grady, "6 Qualities of a True Covenant Friend," *Charisma Magazine*, June 25, 2014, https://charismamag.com/blogs/fire-in-my-bones/6-qualities-of-a-true-covenant-friend/.

15. Richard Innes, "The Power of Applause," actsweb.org, https://www.actsweb.org/articles/article.php?i=1094&d=2&c=6.

16. Steve Cummings, "The Father's Eclipse," Bringing Kingdom, https://bringingkingdom.org/blog/the-father-eclipse.

17. Kathleen Odenthal Romano, "10 Reasons Fathers Are so Important to Their Daughters," Holidappy, May 19, 2016, https://holidappy.com/holidays/10-Reasons-Fathers-are-so-Important-to-their-Daughters.

18. *CSB Tony Evans Study Bible* (Nashville: Holman Bible Publishers, 2019), 207.

19. "Corrie ten Boom quote," Quote Fancy, https://quotefancy.com/quote/789811/Corrie-ten-Boom-Hold-loosely-to-the-things-of-this-life-so-that-if-God-requires-them-of.

20. "Our Heart Is Restless until It Rests in You – Augustine," Crossroads Initiative, July 1, 2021, https://www.crossroadsinitiative.com/media/articles/ourheartisrestlessuntilitrestsinyou/.

21. "H7503 – RĀP̄ Â – Strong's Hebrew LEXICON (NASB20)," Blue Letter Bible, www.blueletterbible.org/lexicon/h7503/nasb20/wlc/0-1/.

22. "School-Age and Pre-Teen Sleep: What to Expect," Raising Children Network, December 5, 2022, https://raisingchildren.net.au/pre-teens/healthy-lifestyle/sleep/school-age-sleep.

23. Eye, "Psalm 127:1 – Life In Vain: Your House," *The 4 Gospels Christian Network Blog*, September 18, 2015, http://the4gospelsblog.blogspot.com/2015/09/psalm-1271-life-in-vain-your-house.html.

24. Eryn Lynum, *936 Pennies: Discovering the Joy of Intentional Parenting* (Bloomington, MN: Bethany House Publishers, 2018), back cover.

25. Elizabeth Fishel and Jeffrey Arnett, "When the Kids Leave Home, What's Next?" Next Avenue, February 14, 2014, https://www.nextavenue.org/when-kids-leave-home-whats-next/.

26. Carolyn Mahaney, *Feminine Appeal* (Wheaton, IL: Crossway Books, 2003), 125.

27. Ibid, 122.

28. Elizabeth George, *A Woman After God's Own Heart: Bible Study Workbook* (Dallas: The Sampson Company, 2004), 64.

29. Bethann Miller, *The Invitation, Keys to Strengthening Your Marriage* (USA: ba.perspectives, 2022), 26.

30. Monica Swanson, "The Best Thing a Mother Can Do for Her Children," The MOB Society, October 9, 2013, https://www.themobsociety.com/20131009best-thing-mom-can-children-love-father-well/.

31. John Piper and Wayne Grudem, *Recovering Biblical Manhood and Womanhood* (Wheaton, IL: Crossway Books, 2006), 53.

32. Jeffery Curtis Poor, "The 4 Types of Love in the Bible," Rethink, June 20, 2022, https://www.rethinknow.org/4-types-of-love-in-the-bible/.

33. Maressa Brown, "When It's Okay to Treat Your Kids Differently & When It's Not," CafeMom, August 5, 2014, http://thestir.cafemom.com/being_a_mom/175545/treating_parenting_kids_differently.

34. Ibid.

35. Simply On Purpose team, "5 Love Languages for Kids: A Simple Guide to Using Love Languages," Simply On Purpose, February 9, 2022, https://simplyonpurpose.org/5-love-languages-for-kids-a-simple-guide-to-using-love-languages/.

36. Brown, "When It's Okay to Treat Your Kids Differently & When It's Not."

37. Laurie Winslow Sargent, "When Personality Differences Lead to Difficulties," Focus on the Family, May 6, 2011, http://www.focusonthefamily.com/parenting/schoolage-children/your-childs-personality/when-personality-differences-lead-to-difficulties.

38. Jonathan Akin, "Is Proverbs 22:6 a Promise for Parents?" CBMW, March 23, 2015, http://cbmw.org/topics/children/is-proverbs-226-a-promise/.

39. Ibid.

40. Jason DeRouchie, "Train Up a Child in the Way He Should Go," Desiring God, September 20, 2016, http://www.desiringgod.org/articles/train-up-a-child-in-the-way-he-should-go.

41. James Lehman, "Your Child Is Not Your Friend," Empowering Parents, https://www.empoweringparents.com/article/your-child-is-not-your-friend/.

42. Dannah Gresh, *Secret Keeper: The Delicate Power of Modesty* (Chicago: Moody Publishers, 2005), 59.

43. Ray Pritchard, "Mighty Oaks and Graceful Pillars: A Prayer for Our Children," Keep Believing Ministries, September 20, 2001, https://www.keepbelieving.com/sermon/2001-09-30-mighty-oaks-and-graceful-pillars-a-prayer-for-our-children/.

44. Ibid.

45. Holman Bible Publishers, *Holman New Testament Commentary* (Nashville: Holman Reference, 2001), 327.

46. Mark Batterson, "Kairos Moments." Catalyst Leader, March 27, 2019, http://beta.catalystleader.com/read/kairos-moments.

47. Eric Metaxas, *Seven Women and Secrets of their Greatness* (Nashville: Nelson Books, 2015), 51.

48. Verna Bowman, "Yester-time Moms," Verna Bowman, May 12, 2012, https://vernabowman.com/yester-time-moms-2/.

ABOUT THE AUTHOR

Jessie is a national speaker, author, leadership trainer, and the founder of More of Him Ministries, the SHE Leads leadership conference, and The Real Mom conference. She also works with LifeWay as one of their You Lead trainers. The author of ten books, she has a passion for helping women experience God's Word for themselves and encouraging them to move into a "wholehearted" lifestyle devoted fully to God.

Jessie and her husband, John, live in Bethlehem, Pennsylvania, and have been married since 1985. They have two daughters and two wonderful sons-in-law. Being a mimi is one of her greatest joys. Most days, you can find Jessie walking her two furry friends, Murphy and Baxter, or playing with her grandchildren. To learn more about Jessie, her books, and her ministry, visit www.moreofhimministries.org.

For autographed books, bulk order discounts, or to schedule speaking engagements, contact:
Jessie Seneca
jessie.seneca@gmail.com
610.216.2730

To order any of Jessie's books, visit
www.moreofhimministries.org

Also available on Amazon

Like us on Facebook and Instagram

www.ingramcontent.com/pod-product-compliance
Lightning Source LLC
Chambersburg PA
CBHW081004140626
46546CB00019B/3240